# SANCTIFIED THROUGH THE TRUTH

*STUDIES IN JESUS' PRAYER FOR HIS OWN: John 17:17-19*

# SANCTIFIED THROUGH THE TRUTH

## THE ASSURANCE OF OUR SALVATION

# Martyn Lloyd-Jones

*Edited by Christopher Catherwood*

CROSSWAY BOOKS • WESTCHESTER, ILLINOIS
A DIVISION OF GOOD NEWS PUBLISHERS

Cover photo: Dick Dietrich

First printing, 1989

Printed in the United States of America

Library of Congress Catalog Card Number 88-71810

ISBN 0-89107-515-1

All Biblical quotations are taken from
the *King James Version*.

# Contents

# 1

## *The Special People of God*

*Sanctify them through thy truth: thy word is truth. As thou hast sent me into the world, even so have I also sent them into the world. And for their sakes I sanctify myself, that they also might be sanctified through the truth (Jn 17 vv. 17–19).*

In order that we may understand that petition offered on behalf of his followers by our Lord on the eve of his death, let me very briefly remind you of the context. Our Lord is about to go to his death on the cross, about to go out of this world back to heaven and to the glory that he had shared with his Father from all eternity, so he prays for these men whom he is leaving behind him in the world and he gives various reasons for praying for them. He reminds his Father of who they are and what they are; then he comes to his particular petitions for them and his first petition is that God should keep them. He says that he has kept them himself while he has been with them and that none of them is lost 'but the son of perdition; that the scripture might be fulfilled'. Now, however, he is going back to God, and his great prayer is that God should keep them from the polluting influence of the world, and especially from the evil – that is, the evil one. When we considered this great first petition,[1] we noticed that our Lord was very careful to put it in a negative form, as we find in the fifteenth verse: 'I pray not that thou shouldest take

---

them out of the world, but that thou shouldest keep them from the evil.' We considered the various reasons that are given here, and in the Scripture everywhere, why we should never pray to be taken out of the world and why it is for our good and for the glory of God and the extension of his kingdom, that we, his people, should be in this world, and should remain here and use our lives to the full while we are left here.

Now here in this seventeenth verse we come to the second petition: 'Sanctify them through thy truth: thy word is truth.' But though I call this the 'second' petition, it is, of course, intimately connected with, and is, in a sense, a continuation of the first. His great desire is that his people should be kept by God, yes, but not by being taken out of the difficulties and problems. How then are they to be kept? And the answer is that they are to be kept by being *sanctified;* not by being taken out of the world, not by the false solution of monasticism— by a desire to quit life somehow or other—that is not God's way of keeping his people. His method is to ask his Father to sanctify them in the way that is illustrated and emphasised here.

We must, therefore, consider this. What does our Lord mean when he prays, 'Sanctify them through thy truth'—or 'in thy truth'—'thy word is truth'? What is 'to sanctify'? We need to be very careful at this point in our definition of the term, because we must interpret it bearing in mind that the same word is used in the nineteenth verse: 'And for their sakes I sanctify myself, that they also might be sanctified through the truth.' In verse 19 our Lord uses exactly the same word about himself as he uses with regard to his followers here. So we must start by arriving at a true definition of what is meant by 'sanctify'.

Now it is generally agreed that there are two main senses in which this word is used throughout the Bible. The first sense of 'sanctify'—and we must always put this one first because it is the one most emphasised in Scripture—is *to set apart for God, and for God's service.* So you will find that this term 'to sanctify' is not only used of men; it is used even of a mountain, the holy mount on which the Law was given to Moses. Mount Sinai was sanctified, it was set apart for a special function and purpose, in order that God might use it to give his revelation of the Law. The word is used, too, of buildings, and of vessels, instruments and utensils, and various things that were used in the Tabernacle and the Temple. Anything that is devoted to, or set aside for God and for his service is sanctified. So, you see, there is a double aspect to this primary meaning of the word. It means, first, a separation from everything that contaminates and perverts, and the second, positive, aspect is that something or someone is devoted wholly to God and to his use.

Now it is quite obvious that the latter aspect is the only conceivable meaning to this term in verse 19. When our Lord says 'and for their sakes I sanctify myself', he means just that, and nothing else. He cannot be referring to inward purification, because he was already perfect. The word means exactly the same thing in John 10:36 where we read, 'Say ye of him, whom the Father hath sanctified, and sent into the world, Thou blasphemest; because I said, I am the Son of God?' When our Lord tells the people that God the Father had sanctified him, and sent him into the world, he means that the Father had set him apart, it is that sense of the word 'sanctify'.

You will find that this primary meaning of the word sanctify is often applied to Christian people. Read, for instance, 1 Corinthians 6:11, where Paul tells the Corinthians that there was a time when some of them were guilty of terrible sin—drinking, adultery, etc. 'But,' he says, 'ye are washed, but ye are sanctified, but ye are justified in the name of the Lord Jesus, and by the Spirit of our God.' You notice he says they are sanctified before he says they are justified. Now with our superficial and glib ideas about sanctification, we always say, 'Justification first and sanctification afterwards.' But Paul puts sanctification first, which means that they have been set apart by God, and taken out of the world. That is the primary meaning of sanctification and in that sense it comes before justification.

Or take 1 Peter 1:2: 'Elect according to the foreknowledge of God the Father, through sanctification of the Spirit, unto obedience and sprinkling of the blood of Jesus Christ'—sanctification comes before the believing, and the sprinkling with the blood and the justification. So in its primary meaning this word is a description of our position. It means that as Christians we are separated from the world. Our Lord has already said that in verse 16—let me emphasise again the importance of watching every single statement in this prayer and noticing the perfect cohesion of it all—'they are not of the world'. Now he says, 'Sanctify them through thy truth.' They have been set apart, he says in effect; set them still more apart: it means this separation from the world. God said to the children of Israel, 'Thou art an holy people unto the Lord thy God: the Lord thy God hath chosen thee to be a special people unto himself' (Deut 7:6). And that is applied in 1 Peter 2:9 to the Christian church: 'Ye are,' it is said again, 'a peculiar people', a special possession for the Lord. It does not mean that the nation of Israel was sinless, but it does mean that they had been set apart as God's peculiar, special people; and the same is true of the church and of all Christian people. We are a holy nation, set apart for God and for his service and for his purpose. That is the primary meaning.

But there is a second meaning and this is equally clear from the Scriptures. This is that we are not only regarded as holy, we are *made holy* and, obviously, we are made holy because that is how we are regarded. God sets us apart as his peculiar people, and because of this we must be a holy people: 'Ye shall be holy: for I the Lord your God am holy,' says God (Lev 19:2). So that we are to be holy because we are holy, and that is the great New Testament appeal for sanctification. So this second meaning is that God does a work within us, a work of purifying, of cleansing, and of purging, and this work is designed to fit us for the title which has been put upon us. We have been adopted, taken out of the world and set apart, and we are now being conformed increasingly to the image, the pattern, of the Lord Jesus Christ; so that we may in truth be the people of God: in reality as well as in name. So this is obviously a progressive work. The first is something that is done once and for all, and it is because we are set apart that we are justified. God has looked upon his people from all eternity and has set them apart—we dealt with that at great length in verses

6, 7 and 8.[1] He sanctified them before the foundation of the world, and it is because of that, that they are justified, and, again, because of that, they are sanctified in this second sense.

So the question is, which of these two meanings is to be attached to the word in the seventeenth verse? It seems to me that there is only one adequate answer to that: obviously both meanings are involved. Let me put it like this: as his followers we are separated from the world—'They are not of the world, even as I am not of the world'—they are separated for God's special service, to represent him in the world. For he says in verse 18, 'As thou hast sent me into the world, even so have I also sent them into the world.' He has already said that he is to be glorified in us and through us; we have been set apart for this special task of glorifying Christ, of bearing the message to an unbelieving world; and because we have been set apart for that, we must be fitted to do it. We must be kept from the evil, and from the tarnishing effect of the world. We must be fit to represent the Father, to proclaim his message and to glorify his dear Son. In other words, this petition is that we should become more and more the special people of God. Our very task and calling demands that we must be a holy people since we cannot represent a holy God unless we ourselves are holy.

Therefore, we are obviously here face to face with the great New Testament doctrine of sanctification. Now I shall not use this as an occasion for giving a full-orbed description and account of that doctrine—although in a sense I shall be doing so, because I shall be dealing with fundamental principles—but at this point we shall deal with the subject solely in terms of what we are told about it in these three verses.

So then, let me give you the divisions as I understand them. We shall not deal with them all in this study, but let me give you the complete outline. Our Lord here deals with three great matters with regard to this subject of our sanctification. First: *Why* does our Lord pray for our sanctification? And a complete answer is given here to that question. The first answer is

---

[1] Volume 2, *Safe in the World* (Crossway Books, 1988)

that he does so because that is the way in which we are to be
kept from the world and from the evil. He also prays for it
because of the task which has been allotted to us (v.18), and
thirdly, he prays for it because the whole object of his going to
the death of the cross is that we might be sanctified—'And for
their sakes I sanctify myself, that they also might be sanctified
... ' (v.19).

The second great matter which is dealt with here is the
*method of sanctification*: 'Sanctify them,' he says, 'through thy
truth'—in thy truth—'thy word is truth.' The way in which
God sanctifies us is obviously vitally important, and our Lord
deals with it here; we are to be sanctified in the truth.

And the third subject with which he deals is the question of
*what it is that ultimately makes our sanctification possible*: and
again he gives the answer in verse 19: 'for their sakes I sanctify
myself.' Without that we never could be sanctified, it would be
quite impossible. So the whole basis of sanctification is ultimately our Lord's action and work on our behalf, supremely
upon the cross.

So let us then start our consideration of this great matter by
dealing with that first question, though we shall not deal with
the whole of it in this study. The first question is, Why does our
Lord pray thus for the sanctification of his followers, indeed, as
he says in verse 20, of all his people, you and me and all Christian people at all times? As we saw, his answer is that he does so
in order that we may be kept from the world and its polluting,
tarnishing effect; and above all that we may be kept from the
evil one. 'I pray not that thou shouldest take them out of the
world, but that thou shouldest keep them from the evil.' And
this is God's way of doing that.

Now we come here to the vital subject of the relationship of
the Christian to the evil which is in this world. It is a subject
which is very often misunderstood, and this has constantly
been so throughout the long history of the church; indeed, I
suggest to you that it is very frequently misunderstood at the
present time. So let me, therefore, put it in what I regard as the
most definite form. What is the relationship of the church, and

of the Christian, to general morality? What is their relationship to measures which are designed to produce and to preserve the overall moral condition of society? What is to be the relationship of the church and the Christian to councils dealing with moral issues, to temperance societies and organisations designed to defend the observance of the Sabbath and things of that kind? There are large numbers of such organisations in the world at this present time. In the light of what we are told here about the relationship of the Christian and the church to the world, and to the polluting effect of evil, it seems to me that we must think about this question, and I would like to put the following consideration to you.

Let me put it first of all in the form of a blunt assertion which I shall proceed to justify. My reply with regard to the relationship of the church and the individual Christian to such matters and organisations is that the Christian's interest in such things is not direct but indirect. Let me put it in this way: all these matters are a part of the function of the state and not of the church as church, nor of the Christian as Christian—of the Christian as a citizen of the state, certainly, but not of the Christian qua Christian.

Let me then show you the value of these things. The functions of the state are of necessity good because the state has been appointed by God; let us never forget that. It is therefore a good thing to point out things which are wrong. Some organisations quote from statistics and show the harmful effect of certain practices; temperance societies, for instance, prove the evil effects of alcohol. Again, some societies are concerned to show that if a man works seven days a week, his work will be less effective than if he works only six. It is a good thing to give the body physical rest and they use that as an argument for Sunday observance. These things are perfectly all right and we should be glad of them and pay due attention to them. Teaching about morality, in and of itself, is right. It is good to warn people against the consequences and the dangers of wrong actions, and it is right that the law of the land should be enforced. It is wrong to break the law, and it should be the business of all citizens to see that the law of the land and of the statute book is enforced.

I want to go further: it is right that the state should enforce God's law, because the state derives its own being from God. Christian people, let us never forget this. The state is not a human contrivance, it is not man who has conceived the idea of the state and of law, it is God who ordained it. God has ordained the bounds and the habitation of every nation; God has called magistrates and the powers that be, and put them into being. I can say, therefore, that as God has organised the state, indeed all the states in the world, it is the business of all to see to it that the state does its work properly. And one of the duties of the state is, therefore, to see that God's name is honoured and glorified, and that God's day is kept.

And my next step is, obviously, that if all that is right, it is therefore the business of the Christian, as a citizen of the state, to see that all that is done. It is not right to say that because a man is a Christian he should have nothing to do with politics or to say that legislation is thoroughly unscriptural. 'Ah,' says someone, 'politics is a dirty game.' But that is the very reason why Christians should speak out, for if God has decreed that the state is the way in which the world should be governed, Christian people should be concerned to see that it is done in the right and true way. One often wonders whether what is so frequently said about national and local politics is not true simply because so many Christian men and women find politics difficult and unpleasant, and are guilty of avoiding it all. It is the business of the citizen to see that the state functions in the best way and one of the functions of the state is to remind men of God, and to see that the rulers are God-fearing people.

But you will see at once that the purpose of all this is simply to set a limit to sin and to the results of sin and wrongdoing. All that I have been describing can do nothing more than control sin and keep it within bounds. I think it is obvious that it is an entirely negative work. All these enactments and all the councils and committees concerned with morality, and the Lord's Day Observance Society, and all these movements, can never make anybody a Christian. It is a very great sin to confuse law and grace. These movements are really only concerned with law, and it is their function to keep people under the law until they come under grace. And that is the right thing to do. People say that you cannot, by an act of Parliament, make a man worship God, but you can prevent him from desecrating God's Day, so you can and should keep him under the law until he comes under grace.

It is because of this, then, that I go on to say that really these laws and regulations and various other things have nothing to do with the Christian as such, and that is why I said earlier on that these things are not primarily the business of the church. That is also why I, as a minister of Christ and as a minister of the church, never speak on temperance platforms. I have never spoken for any one of these organisations designed to observe the Sabbath, nor have I ever spoken on a morality platform. My reason is that it is the business of the church to preach the gospel and to show what I would call, with Paul, 'a more excellent way'. That is why the church must always be very careful to ensure that nothing she does or says should ever detract from or compromise her message and her gospel. The church derives her power entirely and solely from God and in no sense from the state, or from the law. If there is one thing about which we should be more jealous than anything else it is that within the church we recognise no law, no leader, no ultimate king save the Lord Jesus Christ. He is the sole head of the church—no state, no man, no monarch, no one else, but the Lord himself.

The church, in other words, must never hide herself behind the law of the land and she must never try to enforce her message by using the law of the land, for that is to compromise her gospel. It is to make the unbeliever out in the world say, 'Ah these people are trying to force this upon us, they are using the law in order to get it done.' No, at all costs the church must keep her message pure and clean, and she must take her stand upon the purity of the gospel and upon that alone. Indeed I do not hesitate to go so far as to say that the church, claiming as she does that the gospel is the power of God unto salvation, must be prepared to say that her gospel will work in spite of the world, whatever its state, whatever its condition; that even if hell be let loose on the face of the earth, her gospel is still powerful.

'But wait a minute,' says someone, 'don't you think that you ought to see that these other things may help you to preach the gospel? It is an easier thing to preach the gospel to good people than to bad.' As a preacher of the gospel I must reject that. I would query, as a matter of fact, whether it is easier to preach the gospel to good people than to flagrant sinners. I think that historically the opposite is probably true. But apart from historical facts like that, I must stand on the basis that the gates of hell shall not prevail against the church; that as the power of the church is the power of the Holy Spirit, it matters not what the world may be like, for this gospel is the power of God unto salvation, and in order to get right down into the dregs and do its own work, it needs no help from the state. It does not need to hide itself behind the law, because it can stand on its own feet and trust in the power of the living God.

But to look at it a little more particularly, let me put it like this. The Christian, is not sanctified in those ways at all, but in a much more positive way: the gospel way. In sanctification the Christian relies upon the work of God in his soul. 'Sanctify them,' says our Lord, in effect, to his Father. 'It is your work, it is something that, ultimately, you alone can do.' We rely upon God's work, and, of course, this work of God in the soul is regeneration; it is the making of a new man, the creating of a new being, the giving of a new life. So the gospel way of attacking this problem is not negative, like that of the state, but positive.

Let me elaborate that a little by putting it in the form of a few propositions. The gospel and the church are not so much interested in less sin, as in more and positive holiness. All the other movements I have been describing are interested in avoiding sin, but the Christian life is about sanctification. Though a man may refrain from all worldly pleasures, and may never drink, though he may never, even, do any of the things which are wrong in and of themselves, yet, if he does not see himself as a vile, hopeless sinner who is saved only by the shed blood of the Lord Jesus Christ, he is as lost and damned as the most profligate sinner in the world. The church and the Christian should not be interested only, or even primarily, in the general social effects of salvation, but in the fact that men and women should be brought nearer to God, and should live for his glory. When the church gives the world the impression that she is interested in revival only in order to heal certain moral sores, she is denying her own message. I am not primarily interested in revival in order that the streets of our cities may be cleansed; I am interested in it because I believe that for any man not to glorify God is an insult to God. I know that such a man is held bound, and my desire for him is that he may come to know God and glorify him in his daily life. The church is not interested primarily in the social consequences of irreligion. As I read my history, I see that it was because our fathers and grandfathers made that very error, towards the end of the Victorian era, that Christendom is in its present position. They became so interested in social conditions that they forgot this primary truth. They thought that if everybody was kept in order by certain Acts of Parliament, all would be well. But that is morality, and not Christianity.

So let me come to my next proposition. The church, and the Christian, and the gospel, are not so much concerned about removing the occasions for sin, as in removing from man the desire to sin. 'I pray not that thou shouldest take them out of the world, but that thou shouldest keep them from the evil ... Sanctify them ... ' Our Lord is saying, in effect, 'I am not so concerned that you should take the occasion for sin away but that you should take out of man the desire to take advantage of the occasion.' You see the difference? The gospel of Jesus Christ does not so much take the Christian out of the world, as take the world out of the Christian. That is the point. 'Sanctify them': whatever the world is like around and about them, if the world is not in them, the world outside them will not be able to affect them. That is the glory of the gospel; it makes a man free in the midst of hell.

Or again let me put it like this: the gospel is not so much concerned about changing the conditions as about changing the man. Oh the tragedy of the folly and the foolishness that has been spoken about this! They say, 'But surely you must clear up the slums before these people can become Christians?' My friends, one of the most glorious things I have ever seen is a man who has become a Christian in the slums, and then, though remaining in the same place, has transformed his home and house there. You need not change the man's conditions before you change the man—thank God, the gospel can change the man in spite of the conditions.

Do not misunderstand me. I started by saying that it is the business of the state to change the conditions. I am now talking of the function of the church *qua* church, and I would finally put it in this way: our main concern should be not so much to limit the power of evil, as to increase the power of godliness within us. Let me give an illustrataion at this point. The gospel is not primarily concerned to remove the sores of infection, or to put us out of the danger of infection; what the gospel does is to build up our resistance to infection to such a point that it renders us immune to it. The church is not concerned with trying to destroy the infection. Until our Lord returns again the infection will be there; until Satan is cast into the lake burning with fire, the infection will continue. You cannot stop it. It will be there in spite of all your councils and committees. The Christian is not primarily concerned about that. The business of the Christian and the church and the gospel is to see that you and I take so much of the pure milk of the word and the strong meat of the word that our resistance is built up to such an extent that we can, as it were, stay in a house of infectious disease, and be absolutely immune. The germs are there, yes, but we are filled with these anti-bodies that destroy them the moment they attack us.

'Sanctify them'—that is sanctification, and its whole approach is not negative, but entirely positive. Sanctification means that we become like the Lord Jesus Christ. He was so immune that he could sit with publicans and sinners and not be contaminated by them. People could not understand it, the

Pharisees could not understand it. 'This man is a friend of publicans and sinners,' they said. But because of his resistance, our Lord could sit there without danger at all; and what our Lord prays is that we may be made like him. He says, 'As thou hast sent me into the world, even so have I also sent them into the world.' 'Sanctify them.' Make them like me, render them so immune from the assaults of temptation that whenever an attack comes they will always be guarded against it. 'I pray not that thou shouldest take them out of the world, but that thou shouldest keep them from the evil', and that is the ultimate way in which we are kept. We are to be sanctified and holy; we are to become like him, charged with his power and filled with his holiness and righteousness, knowing God and walking with him in the light. And as long as we do that, the world will hold no dangers for us. Though in it, we shall not be of it; we shall be walking through it in the light with God.

# 2

## Sanctification and Evangelism

*Sanctify them through thy truth: thy word is truth. As thou hast sent me into the world, even so have I also sent them into the world. And for their sakes I sanctify myself, that they also might be sanctified through the truth (vv. 17, 18, 19).*

We come now to consider the second great reason which our Lord deduces for praying thus for the sanctification of his people. It is that *our sanctification is absolutely essential to true evangelism.* You notice how he puts it: 'Sanctify them through thy truth: thy word is truth.' Why? Well, 'As thou hast sent me into the world even so have I sent them into the world'—and that is his second reason. Now we must remind ourselves that this question of evangelism is one that applies to us all. I would again point out that in verse 20 our Lord says, 'Neither pray I for these alone'—lest we might think that he was only praying for the apostles – 'but for them also which shall believe on me through their word.' In other words, he includes all Christian people everywhere, always, and at all times and in all places.

It is, therefore, a fundamental teaching of the Scriptures that as Christians we are all saved, not only that we may be safe, but also in order that God may use us in the salvation of others. That is something which is very clear throughout Scripture; it is God's way of evangelising, his way of saving men. He could have adopted other means, but this is the one that he has ordained and chosen, namely, that the work of salvation should

20

be carried on through human instrumentality. This is some-thing that applies to us all; it is not the prerogative or the special work only of those who are called upon to preach. No, it is the task of all the members of the Christian church.

Our Lord has already been saying that in different ways; he has been praying for his followers and has given this as one of his reasons for doing so. He says, 'All mine are thine, and thine are mine, and I am glorified in them' (v.10). It is through Chris-tian people that the Lord Jesus is glorified; that is why he is so concerned about these people. Let us remember that the world knows nothing about him apart from us; it gets to know him through us, and judges him by what it sees in us. Indeed, he puts it still more specifically by saying that even as God had sent him into the world to manifest the glory of God, now he sends his people into the world in exactly the same way, so that he may thus be magnified and glorified through them. So then we must recognise that the plain and clear teaching of Scripture is that every single Christian person is an evangelist.

I think that this is perhaps the thing of all things that needs to be emphasised at this present time. Christianity spread at the beginning, as we see in Acts and in early church history, mainly as the result of the influence of Christian individuals. Their method, above all, was that of cellular infiltration. The com-parison is often made that Christianity spread at the beginning in exactly the same way as Communism is spreading in the modern world; not by holding great mass meetings, but by one person influencing the next person; two people working at a bench and one talking to the other almost unobserved. It is as quiet as the spread of leaven in flour; that is the kind of way it happens. It happened like that in the first century, and it has also happened like that in all periods of true revival and reawakening; the influence of one person upon another. And it seems to me that this is the only hope for the world at the present time, that we shall find again that the Christian message spreads through the influence, the speaking, and the activity of the individual Christian. Our Lord does not argue about this, he just states it: his teaching is that this question of our sanctification is absolutely essential in order that we may truly and properly do that work of evangelism.

We cannot but notice the striking and almost alarming contrast between our Lord's ideas and the modern idea of how this work is to be done. In all the churches and denominations there is a great deal of talk about evangelism; we see it in the newspapers; it is spoken of everywhere. Here are we, facing this question of evangelism, and here is our Lord facing the identical question with regard to his followers: but notice the striking contrast in the approach. As we consider this problem of how the world is to be evangelised, we immediately think in terms of organisations and methods; that, we say, is what is needed. The problem is difficult, so we must now begin to sit down and plan, and set up a number of committees and organisations. Then we must consider how this message can be made attractive. The modern man always tends to think psychologically, so he has to be approached in a particular manner. We must study him, so perhaps it is a good thing to send ministers to work in factories in order that they may know the outlook of the people they intend to evangelise. It is a question of salesmanship and so we study our methods very carefully in order that we may become highly efficient and effective. We want to know what people like, especially the young people. Do they like a certain amount of entertainment? Then they must have it, if it is going to attract them. Then we must get into training, teaching members of the church how to evangelise, we must give them courses of instruction.

There is, therefore, tremendous activity in the Christian church at the present time over this question of evangelism. Our newspapers sometimes comment on it; our religious papers are full of it and all the interest is upon organisation. That, I think you will agree with me, is the attitude of the church today, speaking generally, to the problem of evangelism and evangelisation. But you notice our Lord's method – what a striking contrast! There is the great world, here is a handful of Christian people. They are going to be sent to evangelise that world – how are they to do it? What is the first thing to consider? You notice what our Lord puts first: it is none of the things I have been mentioning. Rather, it is sanctification: sanctify them, for the work needs to be done in them before it can ever be done in the world. Our Lord starts with his own people, and the supreme thing in the matter of evangelism, according to him, is that his followers should be truly sanctified. I do not know what you feel, but there is nothing that appals me so much in the present situation, as the almost incredible way in which Christian people seem to ignore entirely the teaching of the Scriptures with regard to methods of evangelism: the Scriptures might very well never have been written. In the Scriptures, from beginning to end, the method is always the one that is emphasised here. The concentration of the Scripture is upon the messenger, not on his external methods, but on his character and his being, and on his relationship to God.

There are endless illustrations of this. I just select one or two at random. Take the case of Gideon. A mighty enemy army was facing the Children of Israel, and at first Gideon collected an army of 32,000 people. Then God began to reduce them until in the end there were only 300. God in effect said to Gideon, 'I am not going to do this through that great army of 32,000, but in my way.' So he just reduced the 32,000 to 300 and then he sent them out, not with great armaments, but with pitchers with lamps inside them, along with trumpets to blow; and with that ridiculous equipment they conquered the army of the enemy. That is God's way. God has always done his greatest things through remnants. If there is one doctrine that runs through the Scriptures more prominently than any other it is the doctrine of 'the remnant'. How often God has done everything with just one man. You remember the story in 1 Samuel 14 of Jonathan and his armour bearer? They did not spend their time arguing about the condition of the enemy: one man, with his armour bearer, trusting in the living God, could conquer an entire army! It is the great message of Scripture. It is the thing you find constantly in the Prophets. Jeremiah had to stand practically alone in his age and generation. Amos had to do the same thing – that is God's way.

And when you come to the New Testament, what do you find? You find one man, John the Baptist, living in the wilderness, an odd man, and it is through that man that God started this mighty work. Then you go on and read the account of the beginning of the Christian church as we find it in Acts. Judged by our modern ideas and modern methods the thing seems utterly ludicrous. Who were these first disciples, these apostles, these first preachers? Ignorant men, unlearned, untutored, untrained, yet the Lord called them and committed his message and work to such people. He sent them out into that ancient world, and out of this handful, in the hand of God, these mighty things were done. And why? Because they were sanctified, because they were filled with the Holy Spirit. That is what is emphasised here and everywhere; 'not with wisdom of words,' writes Paul to the Corinthians, not with human understanding, but '... in demonstration of the Spirit and of power'; that is the thing that works.

The apostle Paul says of himself—and he tells us that the Corinthians were also saying of him – that his presence was weak, that he had no personality at all, and that he was not a good speaker (1 Cor 2:3; 2 Cor 10:10). Yet it was through a man like that that the gospel first came to Europe and led to those mighty results. It was because the man was sanctified; he was filled with the Spirit of God and God could use him and bring the enemy strongholds crashing down to the ground. Sanctify them, says our Lord, as they face this task of evangelism.

I could very easily go on to illustrate the same thing in the long history of the Christian church. If you read the story of the church throughout the ages, you will find that it has always been like this. Do you realise that the Protestant Reformation came originally from one man, Martin Luther? One man in God's hand can do everything. As an American put it in the last century, 'One with God is a majority'; no matter how many are on the other side. You find that this is the teaching of the Scriptures and this is the teaching throughout the history of the world.

Take one of the most striking examples in modern history,

the great evangelical awakening of 200 years ago. The moral condition of this country was as bad then as it is today. But what happened? What made the change? Well it began with just a handful of men who met together in Oxford to form what they called 'The Holy Club'. These men did not meet together to plan and organise, but to get to know God, to become more holy. Their one desire was to know God better and to be more like him, to be sanctified. So they formed 'The Holy Club' and it was hurled at them as an epithet of abuse—'Methodists'! But that is God's way and it is the only way; it must be the way. God has always done his work like this by separating people, separating them unto himself. That is the meaning of sanctification, God dealing with them and so turning them into instruments that he can use to carry out his work.

This must of necessity be the only way, and here are some of the reasons for this. Our Lord says here that this is the only way of preserving any true unity in the church. The church is only really experiencing unity when she is truly spiritual; this unity is the unity of the Spirit and the bond of peace, not a mechanical unity. The Bible is not interested in external unity. The essential unity that the Bible seeks is that of the Spirit. It is this pure relationship between the various parts of the body that really matters. So it is vital that we should be sanctified, in order that we should have true unity of spirit.

But there is another obvious reason why this is God's way. Evangelism is done through the individual Christian because the man of the world observes the individual Christian. We live in an age when the world tells us—and we must accept its statement—that it is not interested in preaching. But there is one thing the world is always interested in, and that is life and living; and the world today is outside the church for this reason: 'It is all very well for those men to preach, but what happens in practice?' That is what the man of the world says and we must listen to him in this respect. He says, 'I see no point in being a Christian. What have Christian people got that I have not got? Are they more moral? Are they kinder and more loving? Are they less spiteful? Are they less snobbish? What does Christianity do to people who claim to be Christian?' And those are perfectly fair questions. Therefore, the first great step in evangelising is that we should start with ourselves and become sanctified.

Let us imagine that as the result of some great meetings we collect a crowd of people. What are they going to find when they come into the church? Are they going to find something that substantiates the message? If our lives contradict our message there is no point in our preaching or speaking. No, as Peter puts it, in 1 Peter 2:11–12, 'Dearly beloved, I beseech you as strangers and pilgrims, abstain from fleshly lusts which war against the soul. Having your conversation honest among the Gentiles: that, whereas they speak against you as evildoers, they may by your good works, which they shall behold, glorify God in the day of visitation.' You know, he says, that these people are not Christians, and that they are saying all kinds of things against you. Now prove by your life and by your work that they are wrong, and attract them.

Again we know very well that this is something which is not only true in theory but also in practice. When the man of the world sees that you and I have got something that he obviously has not got, when he finds us calm and quiet when we are taken ill; when he finds we can smile in the face of death; when he finds about us a poise, a balance, an equanimity and a loving, gentle quality; when he finds we are immune to the 'slings and arrows of outrageous fortune', he will begin to take notice. He will say, 'That man has got something,' and he will begin to enquire as to what it is. And he will want it. For the modern man, though he may be putting up a bold front, is really unhappy within himself. He wants this 'something'. He does not know what it is, but when he sees it, he is ready to listen. Mere talk, mere preaching alone, is not going to influence him; we must demonstrate these things in our daily life and living.

Let me illustrate this from one actual case. I remember once in a church which I knew very well, I was being entertained by a lady who seemed to be one of the leading lights in the church, and to my astonishment I found that her husband never went near the place at all. I subsequently discovered that the probable

·eason was that the lady, while very active and busy in church work, was failing lamentably in certain practical aspects – she did not always pay her grocer's bill, for example. Yes, she was a great church worker but she was negligent in matters like that. Subsequently this lady, who had only been a nominal Christian, really became a true Christian. And what happened next? Only six weeks after his wife's conversion, and without anyone asking or pleading with him, the husband began to attend that place of worship. He now came because he saw that something had happened to his wife. There was no need for anyone to say anything: he saw the genuine thing, he saw the change in her, and then he began to wonder what had happened and so he came to see for himself. That is sanctification. If Christians are to evangelise the world, they themselves must be right, there must be no contradiction between the message and the life. This is vital, and we know perfectly well that failure here is probably the major reason why so many people adopt a kind of cynicism about the Christian faith and message at the present time. All our elaborate efforts to get people to come to church are going to be useless if, when they come, they find the message contradicted within the church herself.

But, I suppose, the ultimate reason why our sanctification is vital for evangelism is that God can only use people who are sanctified: the vessel must be clean and it must be 'fit and meet for the Master's use'. Let us face the facts: there is nothing that is really going to touch the world as it is today except a mighty revival of the Spirit of God. You may think that I am being pessimistic, but I do not hesitate to prophesy that all efforts and all organisations, whether we invoke the aid of the press or not, will come to nothing. I have watched so many campaigns, and the situation of the church has gone steadily down in spite of them all, and that will continue. Nothing but the operation of the Spirit of God can possibly deal with the situation, nothing else at all; and the Spirit of God works through clean vessels and clean channels. He will not work in any other way. It is so plain and clear, and if only men and women would put all the energy that they are ready to put into organisations, into seeking God and living in his presence and becoming truly sanctified, ther revival would come at once. But we are willing to do anything rather than this; the thing that God puts first is the thing we never mention – sanctification.

So I suggest that if we are concerned about the present state of affairs we must all ask ourselves this question: If my life is not influencing others and bringing them to Christ, why is it not? My friends, you do not need a course of instruction in how to evangelise people – such a thing, were it not tragic, would indeed be ludicrous! Do you think that that was done 200 years ago? Do you think the early Christians attended special coaching classes? Of course they did not! What happened was that they became true Christians and inevitably they were evangelists. When a man has the Holy Spirit within him he does not need instruction, he does it! It has always been like that and we are no different. We are not a special category of Christian. The Christian is the same in every age and generation and the world is always the same. No, we do not need to organise the thing; we need to start with ourselves and to be in such a relationship with God that he can use us. There should be a kind of radiance about us, and something emanating from us, which, when people meet us, makes them say, 'What is it in this man or woman? What is this peculiar, strange thing?' When people are sanctified, they will act as evangelists.

We have seen then that sanctification is necessary to keep us from the evil one, and that it is necessary for evangelism. Now let me say a word about the third great reason which our Lord gives for praying for the sanctification of his people. This is that our sanctification is God's ultimate purpose for us: 'For their sakes I sanctify myself, that [in order that] they also might be sanctified through the truth.' This again is something you find running right through the Scriptures: 'This is the will of God, even your sanctification' (1 Thess 4:3). You notice how explicitly our Lord puts it in his prayer. He says, I am going to the death of the cross, I am going to face that last agony in order that they may be sanctified in truth. 'Who gave himself for us,' says Paul to Titus, 'that he might redeem us from all iniquity, and purify unto himself a peculiar people, zealous of good works' (Tit 2:14). That is why he died on the cross. As the hymn puts it, 'He died that we might be forgiven.' Yes, thank God. But it did not stop there. 'He died to make us good.' And that is what we tend to forget. This is the object of it all, the whole object of the entire work of the Lord Jesus Christ. He came into this world in order that we might be sanctified.

But we have certain dangers to face at this point. May I put it to you like this. The first danger I recognise is that of isolating doctrines, of separating them from one another in a false manner. You know what I mean. It is the danger of separating justification and sanctification in the wrong way. Of course we have to realise intellectually the difference between justification and sanctification, but we must never separate them in practice, and say that I have one without the other. That is absolutely false. According to the Scriptures a man cannot be justified without being sanctified at the same time. Paul puts it like this in Romans 8:30: 'Moreover whom he did predestinate, them he also called: and whom he called, them he also justified: and whom he justified, them he also glorified.' He goes right to the end. Now the danger is that we tend to isolate these things from one another and we tend to say a man can come to Christ and receive his justification, but that he may not come to Christ and receive sanctification until a number of years later. That is utterly impossible, according to the Scriptures, because everything is a part of one plan, and when God starts this movement it goes on inevitably to the end. The moment a man is justified, the process of sanctification has already begun. It is all in Christ. He is 'made unto us wisdom, and righteousness, and sanctification, and redemption' (1 Cor 1:30). He is everything, and you cannot divide Christ. If you have Christ at all you have the whole Christ. But there is a tendency among us to divide these things in a false manner, and to fail to realise that our Lord died upon the cross not only that we might be forgiven, but that we might be made good.

I am talking about the danger of seeking the experience of forgiveness only, without realising that at the same time we should

desire to be holy and to be sanctified. I think that this is very serious. There are so many today who seem to believe that a man
can come to Christ for forgiveness, for happiness, for help, for
encouragement, for guidance and for a thousand and one
things, and yet the whole time they say that he may not receive
the blessing of sanctification. That, they say, may come later
and men are exhorted to come to Christ for one particular blessing, and sanctification is never mentioned at all. Now this,
again, is entirely contrary to the teaching of Scripture. How a
man can possibly come to Christ without being concerned
about sanctification, I cannot understand. How you can read
these descriptions of him in the Gospels, without seeing his holiness and what he had come to do, is indeed beyond my com-
prehension.

In other words, the real danger is that of a false evangelism
that does not include in its preaching the message of sanctification. There is a type of evangelical person who divides these
things up to this extent. They say, 'Yes, Sunday mornings you
edify the saints; Sunday evenings you give to evangelism with
gospel preaching, and, of course,' they say, 'that service means
nothing to the believer, it is for the unbeliever.' But that is not
true evangelism. That is not the evangelism which I find in the
New Testament. It is a false evangelism, and it carries with it a
false modern view of an evangelist as a man who is not much
of a teacher; he may not know much, but he is good at attracting
people. Is that the New Testament picture of an evangelist? Is
that the picture of the evangelist in the church throughout the
centuries? Is that your idea of men like George Whitefield or
John Wesley? The whole thing becomes entirely ludicrous! It is
there I think that we go wrong, right at the beginning. It is our
whole idea of evangelism that is wrong. We seem to think that
the one business of evangelism is to give man a sense of forgiveness and a sense of happiness and joy and peace. But here our
Lord reminds us that there is only one ultimate object in
evangelism and that is to reconcile men to God. It is the whole
end of everything that the Lord Jesus Christ came to do. He
came to reconcile men and women to God: not to give us par-

ticular advice about how to put ourselves in a right relationship to God. 'God was in Christ, reconciling the world unto himself' (2 Cor 5:19), and therefore the message of evangelism must of necessity include the message of holiness.

So what is evangelism? I am not sure but that the first message of evangelism is that we must tell men about holiness. That is the truth which we must preach to men, the truth about this holy God before whom they will have to stand. The business of evangelism is to tell them that there is one way in which they can stand in the presence of God and that is by being made holy. It is not enough for them to have a sense of forgiveness; the question is, Are they fit to stand in the presence of God? Without holiness they cannot: 'holiness, without which no man shall see the Lord' (Heb 12:14). So an evangelism that does not include that as an integral part of its message is not biblical evangelism. The whole problem with us is that we have all become so subjective, so influenced by modern thought, that we always start with ourselves instead of starting with God. I am unhappy; I want happiness. I want this or that, so I will go to this or that religious meeting in order that I may have what I want; and I get it and stop at that. But, my dear friends, the place to start is right at the other end. It is with *God*. God is, and we are all in his hands and we all have to face him. The first question that we should put to every man is not, 'How do you feel, are you happy or miserable?' No, it is, 'How are you going to stand in the presence of God?' And if we start with that question, it is inevitable that this matter of sanctification is bound to come in. If I stand and face men and ask them how they are going to meet God, I cannot do it flippantly; I cannot do it lightly and glibly. There must be a holy seriousness about the matter. One is appalled when one thinks what is going to happen to the godless and the unbeliever. We must start with God, and if you and I claim to be Christians, the claim we are really making is that we are God's people, his representatives, and that we are going to tell people about God and are going to bring people to him.

Surely it is clear that we can only do so as we ourselves are God-fearing, as we are godly, as we are like the Lord Jesus

Christ himself. He came to this world to be the 'first born among many brethren', and we are formed and fashioned after his image. A Christian, by definition, is one who is to be like Christ. Therefore our Lord prays, 'Sanctify them,' make them like me, so that you can use them to glorify yourself among men and women in the world. So the beginning of everything is a right concept of holiness, the holiness of God, for without that we shall avail nothing.

# 3

# 'For Their Sakes'

*And for their sakes I sanctify myself, that they also might be sanctified through the truth (v. 19).*

We have been dealing with the reasons which our Lord adduces for praying for the sanctification of his followers. One is that this is God's way of dealing with his people, and the second reason, which we considered in our last study, is the vital importance of this from the standpoint of evangelism. We went further and saw that this is in reality the end and object, the ultimate, in the whole matter of salvation. We saw therefore that to consider salvation apart from sanctification is false.

But now we come to another aspect of this subject, which is *the basis of sanctification;* indeed to the only way in which our sanctification is at all possible, to the very foundation of it. We find it here, in one of the most glorious statements which can be found anywhere in the Scriptures: '... for their sakes I sanctify myself.' I know that I often say about various phrases like this in Scripture, that it is incomparable and that there is nothing like it; and of course every time one says that, it is perfectly true, because so many of these statements, containing as they do the very essence of the gospel, are indeed incomparable. Furthermore, the Holy Spirit applies these statements to us from time to time so that, as any particular one is applied to us, it does seem to us at that moment to be all we need, and then at another time the same is true of another statement. So there is no contradiction in saying that both of them, and all of them, are equally incomparable. Here, then, is surely one of the greatest and most glorious statements in the whole range of Scripture. It is like a gem with many facets; it does not matter from which angle you look at it, it shines still more brightly and wonderfully. It is at the same time, surely, one of the most vital statements that we can ever consider together. So let me hold this glittering jewel before you, praying that nothing in our study will in any way detract from its brightness and glory. The whole of the Christian gospel is in this one phrase: 'For their sakes I sanctify myself.'

Now the first thing that must engage our attention is obviously the meaning of Christ's sanctification of himself. Clearly, as we pointed out earlier when we began to consider this doctrine, he cannot mean that he will do anything to increase his own holiness. That is impossible. He was perfect from the beginning, without blemish, without sin and without fault, so that when he says that he is going to sanctify himself he cannot mean that he is going to make himself more holy than he was before. What it means, obviously, is that he is using the term in the primary sense of sanctification, namely dedication, consecration, a setting apart for the special work of God, and for God's purpose in him and through him. It means an entire offering of oneself to God for his glory and for his purpose.

Then, in order to grasp the full meaning of this statement, the next word we must look at is 'myself' – 'I sanctify myself,' our Lord says. And by that he clearly means himself as he is in his total personality, everything that he is, as God and man, all his powers, all his knowledge, all his perfection, all his ability, everything. There is no word more inclusive than this word 'myself'. It means my total self, all that I am, in and of myself, all my relationships, all my privileges, all my abilities and all my possessions. I sanctify myself in the full totality of my being and my personality. So what our Lord is really saying at this point is that all that he is and has, he is now giving entirely and utterly to God 'for their sakes' – they being the Christians then in existence; and for our sakes, too, those who are going to come

into existence; all those people he has been talking so much
about in this prayer, the people who had been given to him by
God, and for whom he has come into the world, and for
whom he is now doing everything: 'for their sakes I am giving
my total self to you'.

This is, ultimately, the very acme of Christian doctrine and
it is astonishing to notice how we tend to forget it. I suppose
it is one of those truths we forget because we think we know
it, and we tend to take it for granted. We are inclined to stop
at certain particulars in the work and actions of our Lord, not
realising that the greatest thing of all, the staggering fact, is
that the Lord Jesus Christ, the Son of God, has devoted himself entirely to our redemption. He has given himself up in the
totality of his personality to this one specific object. Now that,
it seems to me, was the thing that was done in the Eternal
Council between God the Father, God the Son and God the
Holy Spirit, before the world was ever created. All the history
of mankind was known, everything was clear and open, the
whole course of man, his life and his history. Before the foundation of the world, the Fall, the sin and shame were all fore-
seen, and what our Lord is really doing here is repeating,
reminding God, as it were, that in the Eternal Council he had
turned to the Father and said, 'Here am I, send me.' I put
myself entirely in your hands, at your disposal, you can use
me as you like for the redemption of this people. He sanctified
himself, he devoted himself, to this task. He leaves everything
else and he excludes everything else.

We are familiar with that idea on a lower and lesser level.
We know, for instance, that when a man joins the army to
fight for his country he has to give up certain other things. He
gives up his business, or profession, for the time being. He has
to give up his home and family life. The man is now devoting
and consecrating himself to the service of his country, in order
to defend it. He is a man who is giving himself exclusively to
this one task and it means giving up something else. And the
Scripture teaches that that is precisely what the Lord Jesus
Christ has done for us and for our redemption. When he says

here, 'I sanctify myself,' he is going to do something, and it is very important that we should be quite clear what he means.

There is a sense in which he has already done this; as we have seen, a great promise was made before the foundation of the world in the Eternal Council. But then it was put into practice at the Incarnation; the very birth of our Lord into this world was a part of the sanctifying of himself to this one task of man's salvation. Even at that particular point it involved his laying aside the signs and marks of his eternal glory and Godhead. He did not lay aside his Godhead, that was something he could not do. (That was the false doctrine about 'self-emptying' which came in about sixty or seventy years ago.) No, he did not empty himself of his Godhead, but he certainly did empty himself of some of the prerogatives of his Godhead.

That is the great statement made by Paul in Philippians 2:5–8: 'Who, being in the form of God, thought it not robbery to be equal with God', which means that he did not regard his equality with God as a prize to be held on to, or to be clutched at. He is devoting himself to this peculiar task, so for the purpose of this task he lays aside the marks and the signs of his glory; as the hymn puts it, 'Mild he lays his glory by'. Now that is a part of this sanctification of himself. He laid aside the signs of his glory and he submitted to being born as a babe in weakness and in utter helplessness.

So, then, he had offered himself to the Father and he said, I am going to make myself responsible for the salvation of these people and I care not what it may cost. I give myself entirely to this task. He left the courts of heaven, and took upon himself human nature, which meant that he became man as well as God. He was fashioned in the likeness of man and came into the world as a man among men – that, too, is a part of the sanctification of himself, of setting himself apart for this task. He then lived that extraordinary life for thirty years, apparently nothing but man, working as a carpenter, sharing the life of ordinary people. He so humbled himself that he became liable to temptation by Satan. God cannot be tempted, we read, but here is God in the flesh being tempted by the devil; and all this is part of his setting himself apart. Before he could save mankind, he had to endure this, and so he was tempted in all points like as we are, yet without sin.

It was also a part of his preparation for his high priesthood. You remember that argument in Hebrews 4:15, 'For we have not an high priest which cannot be touched with the feeling of our infirmities.' Because of what he endured and suffered, he was being made perfect as 'the Captain of their salvation' (Heb 2:10) – because he endured temptation by the devil and the contradiction of sinners against himself, and lived an ordinary life in this world.

But now he turns to the Father and he says that he is going to do something even further and deeper than that. What I have been describing is tremendous and staggering, but now there is something glorious! He is now giving himself to God to be made the actual sin-bearer, the offering for sin. He has come down from heaven, he has identified himself with us. He submitted himself to baptism though he never committed a sin, identifying himself with us sinners. He has endured all that I have described, yes, but if man is to be sanctified, if man is to be made so that he can dwell with God and dwell with him to all eternity, something further has to be done. So he gives himself to that something further. He hands himself passively to the Father and he says, I am ready now to be made sin for them. I am here offering myself for their sins; lay their sins upon me, make me their sin-offering. He handed himself over – that is what is meant by sanctification. He made a further devotion of himself, the last act of consecration.

Let me put it in the language of Scripture. He has submitted himself to be made a curse for us: 'Cursed is everyone that hangeth upon a tree' (Gal 2:3, quoting Deut 21:23). To be crucified was to be cursed, it was a fearful disgrace, and here he says to his Father, in effect, 'As this is the only way whereby they can be sanctified, I give myself and I make myself a curse. Let their sin really come upon me that they may be sanctified. I hand myself over to this.' It is simply saying what he said in another way, in the Garden of Gethsemane, 'Father, if it be possible, let this cup pass from me: nevertheless not my will but thine be done'; if there is no other way, I will take the cup and drink it to the dregs. He is setting himself apart into the hands of God for this end and object.

He is now submitting himself, therefore, to the most terrible thing that he ever contemplated, namely that he should be separated from his Father. He had come out of the eternal bosom. He was in God from the beginning, he is co-equal, and co-eternal with God; but here he realises, and he faces it, that in order to save and to sanctify these people he has to undergo this separation from God and to be made a curse. It means the breaking of the contact, and he submits himself even to that. He is prepared to endure even the loss of the face of God on the cross that we might be sanctified. He separates himself to this.

For that is what he endured on the cross; our Lord died of a broken heart. Christ's heart was literally broken, which is why they found blood and water when they thrust the spear into his side. He did not die merely as a result of physical crucifixion, that was not the thing that killed him. His heart was broken. The authorities, you remember, were somewhat surprised when they found him dead already. Usually crucifixion is such a slow death that men had to be killed when they were crucified: the thieves had their legs broken (Jn 19:32–33). But he died quickly, because he bore the punishment of our sin. He endured your hell and mine. This was no mere appearance, but something that was done. He endured our suffering, he consecrated himself to that. He says, Here I am, pour out the vials of your wrath because of the sin of these people upon me. I hand myself over that you may do it. 'For their sakes I sanctify myself, that they also might be sanctified through the truth.'

And then he sets himself apart for death, for burial, for entering into Hades. He descends into Hades (however we may interpret that) in its fullness and entirety. But it does not even stop at that. I think that Scripture teaching shows very clearly that our Lord's setting himself apart for this great end and object goes even beyond death and the grave; it is a part of his resurrection. For when the Lord Jesus Christ rose again from the dead, he rose not merely in and of himself, but also as the representative of his people. Even now his life in heaven is not a life he lives for himself – I say it with reverence – it is primarily a life that he is living for us, his people. He is our Advocate, our High Priest, our representative in the presence of the Father. The Lord Jesus Christ at this moment is peculiarly engaged in the work of the kingdom of which you and I are citizens. He shall reign 'till his enemies be made his footstool' (Heb 10:13).

Oh what high doctrine we are handling here! The Lord Jesus Christ in heaven at this moment, is not the same as he was when he left heaven, to come to earth. When he did that he left it as God, God the Son, but when he returned to heaven he was God and Man. He has taken human nature with him. He is God and Man for ever and for ever; the head of the church, the representative of his people. And the astounding teaching seems to be that he has set himself apart even in the Godhead to this particular work for his people and for his church; that is the thing to which he devotes himself entirely.

So the doctrine can be put like this: he who was co-equal and co-eternal with the Father has come within the bounds of time and has lived a human life here on earth. He has set himself exclusively to this one task: 'From the highest throne of Heaven to the Cross of deepest woe, all to ransom guilty captives ...' That is it; it is all there in these wonderful and magnificent words of our passage. I wonder whether we grasp this, whether we realise what it truly means that this second blessed person in the holy eternal Trinity, brought himself out, as it were, and exclusively gave himself to this one, peculiar task. All that has happened to him, and all that he has done and all that he is doing is designed to this end and object. 'For their sakes I sanctify myself.' That is what it meant to him, and that is what it involved for him.

From all this I deduce, therefore, that clearly it was all absolutely necessary before you and I could be sanctified.

Every part and every step of it was essential. You and I can only be sanctified because the Incarnation is a fact; we can only be sanctified because the suffering and death, the resurrection and the risen life of our Lord were all facts. We must not leave out any one step; we are not only sanctified by the risen Lord, his death was equally essential, and so too was the Incarnation. One of the most subtle errors at the present time is to say that our sanctification is only in the risen, living, Christ, without the death being mentioned at all. It is a denial of vital, essential, New Testament teaching – every step, every movement, every action was a part of this sanctification of himself, and without this we cannot be sanctified.

That, then, leads us to the practical application: how does all this lead to our sanctification? 'For their sakes I sanctify myself, that they also might be sanctified through the truth.' How does it work? Well, as I understand this New Testament doctrine, we can put it like this. Everything is in the Lord Jesus Christ. Everything that we enjoy, everything that we ever shall be, is because of our relationship to him. We are in him, and he is in us. We are parts of him, and we are sharers, therefore, of all that he is. All that he has done, he has done for us as our representative. Therefore all that belongs to him belongs also to us, and by his sanctification of himself he has made our sanctification possible.

It works out in this way. Before you and I could ever be sanctified, the barrier of sin between us and God had of necessity to be removed. Sanctification ultimately means being like God, sharing the life of God, being in the right relationship with God and having perfect communion with him. Sanctification does not just mean being rid of certain sins. No, sanctification is positive. God says, 'Ye shall therefore be holy, for I am holy' (Lev 11:45). But before that is possible it is quite clear that the barrier and obstacle between us and God must be removed. That is why the cross of Calvary is absolutely essential to sanctification, and people who say that we can be sanctified by knowing the living Christ, without talking about the Atonement, have clearly not understood the problem of sin. Sin must be taken out of the way. The first question is the guilt of our sin, and it is only by the death of our Lord upon the cross, by his making himself our sin-bearer, and becoming the sin-offering, that the guilt of sin can thus be taken out of the world. So he tells us here that he is offering himself in order that that may be done. It is the very foundation of sanctification. Justification is the basis of sanctification in this second sense of the word.[1] And that is the error of the Roman Catholic Church when they fail to emphasise the doctrine of justification by faith only; men and women try to sanctify themselves by going into monasteries and so on, and of course it cannot be done, for without justification there can be no sanctification. Sin must be removed, and our Lord has removed it.

Then the next thing that happens is that in him we are reconciled to God. Sin has been taken out of the way, the guilt has been removed, and now God, in a marvellous manner, puts us into Christ; he incorporates and engrafts us into him. As you read the New Testament, keep your eye on that phrase 'in Christ'. Paul talks about certain men and says that they were 'in Christ before me' (Rom 16:7). He had been put into Christ, like a branch being grafted into a tree. We are members of the body of Christ, adopted as God's children, taken into God's family – that is the New Testament language – and if Christ had not set himself apart for us, that would never have been done. He is 'the first born among many brethren', the beginning of a new humanity. He is starting a new race of man, and we who are put into him become the beneficiaries of everything that is true of him. We are received by him, and thus we receive new life from him. We receive a new nature, we become partakers of the divine nature, and we become such that the very Holy Spirit that was given to him without measure can be given to us also. We can be enabled to live life in this world in the way that he

[1] See chapter 1 for a discussion of the two meanings of sanctification. (Ed.)

lived it. That is what we are taught. We receive the gift of the Holy Spirit himself. He enters into us and dwells in us, and he begins to form Christ in us. We are made according to the image and pattern of Christ – we are created anew in Christ Jesus.

Now all that could never have been if our Lord had not set himself apart for the birth, the death, the entering into Hades, the resurrection, the seating of himself at the right hand of God, and the sending forth of the Holy Spirit. He has done all this in order thatthat might happen to us, and thus it is that the Holy Spirit works within us, both to will and to do according to God's good pleasure. Let me remind you of Paul's argument in Philippians 2:12–13, 'Work out your own salvation with fear and trembling. For it is God which worketh in you' – he does it through the Spirit – 'both to will and to do of his good pleasure.' The moment the Holy Spirit enters into us, then he begins to work in us. Sometimes when we are quite unconscious of it, he creates desires in us and works upon the will – 'to will and to do'. He empowers us, and he does so because Christ has sent him for that purpose. Thus he links us more and more to Christ, forming Christ in us all the time. Ever increasingly we are enabled to receive of his fullness and 'grace for grace'; power, life – every need can be satisfied. The fullness of the Godhead is included, for all the treasures of wisdom and grace are in Christ and if I am put into Christ then I can receive all that; his life will flow into mine, as the branch takes from the vine. The New Testament is full of this teaching but all I am emphasising here is that if he had not sanctified himself, none of this would be possible, and that is why he had to do it. This is our sanctification, and what he says here again is that he has done it all in order that we might be sanctified in truth.

I cannot leave this wonderful statement without just saying a final, brief word about the amazing thing that led him to do all this. It is all here! 'For their sakes I sanctify myself.' If only we could see this. This is the thing that leads to sanctification. We shall be considering this further, but this is the truth that we need to know; we need to realise something of what this means. 'For their sakes,' he says, he is going to do all that I have been describing to you. Who then are they? Who are these people for whom he does it? Enemies of God and therefore enemies of Christ, self-willed creatures, people who listen to Satan rather than to God, people who deliberately believe the lies against God, people who have set themselves up, and put their own wills and desires against the will of God, people who delight in evil, who are full of malice, envy, lust and passion; you and I as we were in sin and in evil, as the result of the Fall.

For *their* sakes! Recognise it, guilty sinners as we are! It is for us that he has done all this – for them, yes, I sanctify myself, says the eternal Son of God, the holy and pure one, the blameless and spotless, the one whose supreme joy was to do the will of his Father. Can you imagine a greater contrast than that: the contrast between 'them' and 'I'? And yet he says, 'I sanctify myself,' which not only means, as I have described to you, the totality of his personality, but also that he did it voluntarily and willingly. There was nothing in us to recommend this; there was no motive that could arise from anything in us. Man in sin is so damned and hopeless that he does not want to be saved, or even ask to be. No request ever went out from man to God for salvation, it has come entirely from God. Here am I, says our Lord, Send me. There was no compulsion from the Father's side, the Son desired to do this. He gave himself freely and willingly and voluntarily.

I do not suppose it is seen more clearly anywhere than it is there in the Garden of Gethsemane. 'If it be possible, let this cup pass from me.' But if it is not possible, if there is not another way, then I will do it. I will go through with it, though I know what it is going to mean.

The agony of it was so great in anticipation that it made him sweat drops of blood, but he willingly went to the shame and agony and all the suffering, the mocking, the spitting, the jeering and the laughter, the crown of thorns. Yes, he willingly went and endured it all for *your* sake, for *my* sake, not simply that we might have our sins forgiven, but that we might be sanctified.

# 4

# *God's Work through the Truth*

*Sanctify them through thy truth: thy word is truth (v. 17).*

Now we come to what I have described in our analysis of this subject as the *method of sanctification*. Our Lord puts it like this: 'Sanctify them through thy truth [or, in thy truth]: thy word is truth.' This is his method of sanctification. We are thus bound to ask this question: How can we become truly holy, how can we become sanctified in truth? Our Lord says, 'For their sakes I sanctify myself, that they also may be sanctified through the truth.' This is not a spurious sanctification, it is real. So, to put it another way, How can we become truly and entirely devoted to God and to his service? How, indeed, can we become like our Lord? He was fully devoted to his Father. He gave himself, he consecrated himself utterly. He was entirely at the disposal of his Father and that is why the Father could use him to bring to pass this great salvation that we enjoy. How, then, can we become as he was? This is obviously a crucial question for all Christian people. I do not hesitate to make the assertion that unless a person is concerned about this question, he or she is not a Christian at all. For it is an essential part of the definition of a Christian that he should be concerned about this matter of becoming wholly and truly devoted to God.

It is not surprising, therefore, that in the long history of the church there have been many different views with regard to the method of sanctification. It is, in a sense, the whole story of the church. A book called, *The Vision of God* by K. E. Kirk gives a very good historical survey of this doctrine. It is a massive book, and one of the most rewarding that I have read on this particular subject. What Kirk does there is to trace historically the two main schools of thought with regard to this question of how one can become holy.

In the one school are the people who believe in the monastic idea that the only way to become holy is to clear right out of the world and to give yourself to nothing but the cultivation of your soul and the development of holiness. Then those in the other school believe that all this can be done in the world as one follows one's ordinary profession and calling among men and women – what might be called the evangelical conception of the method of holiness. Kirk's book is well worth reading, but when all is said, there is still much confusion about this matter and a great deal of perplexity and disagreement.

It is quite a popular thing today to say that it does not matter what you believe about the method of obtaining sanctification as long as it gives you an experience that makes you happy and seems to promote your holiness. There are many who take this view. 'Why be bothered?' they say. 'Why not let one man become a monk if he likes and another man go on with his work in the world? Why not let one man believe that holiness is to be received as an experience and another man believe that it is something which a man has to work out for himself? What does it matter? Why bother about this as long as each man is happy in his own particular way?'

Now it seems to me that such a statement must of necessity be wrong, because if you adopt that line of argument then you have nothing whatever to say to the cults. For whatever we may think about them, if our only test is that of experience, then the cults really do seem able to offer what is required. Yet we would not for a moment grant that they are right, or that the experience they claim is true, because the cults say that they do not believe the truth.

In other words, there must be an objective test for what we believe. Experience is not a test; a man may become very happy and live a much better life than he did before, though he believes something that is not true. The things which are not true in and of themselves may at first appear to do us good because, of course, the devil can turn himself into an angel of light: it is pathetic to notice the way in which people forget that teaching. We must never base our doctrines upon experience, but upon the truth. That is the main reason for not accepting this attitude of letting any man believe what he likes. The Scripture tells us to prove the truth. 'Evil communications corrupt good manners,' writes Paul, to the people in the church at Corinth. You must not say, he tells them in 1 Corinthians 15, that it is irrelevant whether a man believes in the resurrection or not. It does matter, and if men hold a wrong view, eventually it will lead to something wrong in their behaviour. Our duty, therefore, as Christian people is to discover, as far as we can, the teaching of the Scriptures. Obviously we do not do that in a controversial spirit, since controversy for its own sake is always the work of the devil. Remember, however, that the opposite to that is not to say, 'Believe anything you like as long as it helps you.' Rather it is to 'search the Scriptures'. So it is our duty to discover, if we can, what we are told in Scripture about this important and vital matter of the method of sanctification and we do so now in terms of our Lord's teaching at this point in the seventeenth chapter of John.

The first principle, I think we would all agree, is that *this is primarily and essentially God's work in us.* Now the very way in which our Lord puts it, his petition itself, I think, proves that. He is praying to God the Father and he is asking him to do something, and he says, 'Sanctify them'; I plead with you to sanctify these people through the truth. Sanctification, therefore, is essentially and primarily something that God does to us and in us and for us. So it follows that we must never think of sanctification as something which you and I decide to go in for. We must realise that it is always the work of God. We have seen already that the ultimate object of God in the whole process of salvation is our sanctification. That is the end he has in view, the thing which is being brought to pass, and that is the basic principle to which we must always hold. Whatever particular views we may hold about details, we must never forget that, apart from you and me altogether, it is something God does to us. So the main emphasis must never be put upon our deciding to go in for sanctification.

Therefore I would put it like this: sanctification is something that starts within us from the first beginning of the work of grace in us for salvation. There is surely nothing which is more fatal than to separate justification and sanctification completely, and to tell a man that he can be justified without being sanctified, or that you receive your justification at one point, and, perhaps a long time later, you receive your sanctification. The very definition of justification means that that is quite impossible. No man can be justified without his realising that he is a sinner, that he is guilty before God, and that he is exposed to God's wrath and punishment. He desires to get rid of the sin which has put him in that position, to repent and turn from sin and the world, to be put right with God. And the moment a man has realised and said all that, he is giving evidence of sanctification, because sanctification is the process of delivering us from sin in its every aspect. So our justification is proof of the commencement of the process of sanctification, because any dislike of sin, any realisation of what sin cost the Lord Jesus Christ, any movement away from it, however small, is evidence of sanctification. So it does seem to me to be utterly unscriptural to divide these two things and put them into separate compartments, and to say that a man can have one without the other.

Now the way to get out of that difficulty and to avoid that dangerous error, is to realise that the whole work of salvation is God's work, and that every step and movement in God's work of salvation is to bring us to this sanctified, holy position. It is all the work of God from beginning to end. That is why St Paul in Philippians 2:12–13 says, '… work out your own salvation with fear and trembling. For it is God which worketh in you both to will and to do of his good pleasure.' Indeed, he has already said the same thing earlier in the same epistle when he says: 'Being confident of this very thing, that he which hath begun a good work in you will perform it until the day of Jesus Christ' (Phil 1:6).

That is the only true biblical conception of salvation; it is God working in us. God is at work the moment a man even begins to become conscious of sin within himself. God has begun a good work and he is going on with it, and it is all ultimately a part of this matter of sanctification. Therefore we must never think of it in terms of something we decide to 'go in for' or 'take up'. We must realise that God is leading us on in this matter of sanctification, and this can never be over-emphasised. The New Testament makes it so plain that the whole of the work of salvation is God's work in us. A good way of looking at it is like this: we would all agree that in the matter of our justification God has done a lot of work in us even when we did not realise it. Look back across your experience. What was it that ever made you go to that place of worship where you were converted? Do you not see, as you look back, that God was working in you without your realising it? He was bringing certain forces to bear upon you. He brought you face to face with certain people. It seemed accidental at the time – you did not know why you were acting as you did. But the answer is that God was bringing it to pass. No man would come to that point of repentance and belief and faith in Christ were it not that God had been dealing with him, even if the man himself were quite unconscious of it. Now it is exactly the same with regard to this matter of sanctification. He is working in us and upon us, he is doing things to us, and the end and the object of all this is that we may become holy and truly sanctified.

I do not know what you feel, but to me this is my final comfort and consolation in this world. My only hope of arriving in glory lies in the fact that the whole of my salvation is God's work. I therefore know that if I am a child of God, God will complete the work that he started in me. I can never face God and stand in his glorious presence unless I am faultless and blameless. But the practical question is, How am I going to get to that position? I repeat, my only hope and comfort is that, in the last analysis, it does not depend upon me but upon God himself. If I am a child of God and if he has put his hand upon me, then I know for certain that he is going to bring me to that.

And, let me emphasise this very solemnly, Scripture teaches us that God is so determined to bring us to that position, that if we are not prepared to be led by him, he has other methods of bringing us to it. The teaching of the Hebrews 12:6 is: 'Whom the Lord loveth he chasteneth, and scourgeth every son whom he receiveth.' If you are not being chastened, says the author, 'then are ye bastards, and not sons.' It is a terrifying thought and yet it is very comforting. If you are God's child, then God is going to perfect you. If you will not listen to positive teaching, he will chastise you, he will lay his hands upon you. Perhaps your health will suffer or the health of a dear one; there may be an accident, a calamity, a death – the Bible is full of such teaching. God's children are not allowed finally to go astray. He brings them back, if not by one way, then by another. My sanctification is in his hands and thank God it is, for if it were left to me it would be altogether hopeless.

That is another way of presenting Paul's argument in Romans 8: 'Whom he called, them he also justified: and whom he justified, them he also glorified' (v. 30). If God has started this work in us, he is certainly going to finish it and that is our only hope and consolation. Therefore we can say, as Paul does, that we are 'persuaded, that neither death, nor life, nor angels, nor principalities, nor powers, nor things present, nor things to come, nor height, nor depth, nor any other creature, shall be able to separate us from the love of God, which is in Christ Jesus our Lord' (vv. 38–39). So my comfort and consolation is not that I am anxious to be holy and sigh for sanctification, no, my comfort and consolation is that God has set me aside for sanctification, has chosen me unto sanctification, and because he has done so, he is going to do the work.

Or, I can put it like this: my only hope of seeing God and of entering glory is that the Lord Jesus Christ has prayed to God to sanctify me – not that I decide to surrender myself, or to do

this, that and the other, but that Christ himself is asking the
Father to sanctify me. That is my assurance, that is my comfort. I know that Christ's prayer for his own is always infalli-
bly answered, and it is because I know that I am in God's
hands and that God is dealing with me, that I know that ultimately I shall be fit to stand in his holy presence. That then is
the first great principle. It is God's work in us, and he does it
through Christ who has consecrated and sanctified himself,
and has suffered my punishment, and has risen for my justification, and has sent the Spirit in order that I may be
sanctified.

So then we must now go on to consider how God does this
work of sanctification in us. 'Father sanctify them'; I plead
with you to sanctify them. Yes, but how does God do this?
The answer is in the rest of the statement: 'Sanctify them
through [or in] thy truth.' And then our Lord analyses and
emphasises it: 'Thy word is truth.' So the second principle is
that *God's way of sanctifying us is through the medium of
truth, through his word, which is truth.* God's method of
sanctification is that he brings us into a certain relationship to
his truth and to his word. He brings us into the realm of the
truth, into a knowledge of the truth, so that it is the truth of
God working in us that produces our sanctification.

Now that seems to me to be the essence of the method, and
again, of course, this is of vital importance. It is at this point
that disagreement tends to come in. How does God do this
work in us? Let me suggest certain negatives to you, which I
regard as of great importance. The first is that God does this
work of sanctification in us but not in the sense that he does it
all for us so that all we have to do is to keep on looking to
him. I am sure that you are familiar with this teaching. People
say that if God is the one who produces your sanctification,
then, obviously, you do nothing. The greatest hindrance to
the work of God, they say, is that you repeatedly try to do
something for yourself, whereas all you have to do is to surrender yourself to him, and look to him, and as you do so, he
will do the work for you. Then the illustration of the branch

and the vine is used to support this view.

But that seems to me to be an entire contradiction of what our Lord says in his prayer at this point. He prays that God may sanctify us in, or through, the truth. It is a great body of truth that we are going to consider, and that does not mean that we do nothing. Surely the whole illustration of the branch and the vine is sadly misunderstood at that point. The branch in the vine is full of life, and full of its own activity. Of course, it must be in communication with the parent trunk, with the tree itself, but it must not be thought of as a kind of tube through which the sap flows and which contributes nothing of itself. The picture is of an active, living relationship in which the branch has its own function in the work which it carries out, though always in fundamental relationship to the trunk. And that, surely, is the teaching of Scripture. Go back once more to that great statement in Philippians 2:13 '... it is God that worketh in you,' says Paul, 'both to will and to do ...' Yes, but because of that, this is what he says: 'work out your own salvation with fear and trembling.' He exhorts them to work it out because it is God who is working in them. God gives the power whereby we are enabled to work for ourselves; that is the method. So though sanctification is fundamentally the work of God, it does not mean that I do nothing at all but look to him. No, he works in me in order that I may work.

Furthermore, Scripture does not teach that this process of sanctification is a very simple one. Someone once said, 'It is all so perfectly simple, and Christian people give themselves such a lot of trouble because they will make these complications. It is as simple as lifting up a blind and letting the sunlight come into the room. All you have to do, therefore, is to surrender to Christ, and look to him and it all happens to you, and the work of sanctification goes on.'

But Scripture, surely, is full of exhortation. It tells us to rend our hearts (Joel 2:13) and to 'be dead unto sin' (Rom 6:11). It says, 'mortify your members which are upon the earth' (Col 3:5) and mortify the flesh. It tells us to 'stand fast in the faith' (1 Cor 16:13) and to have faith in God. It tells us to 'flee these things' (1 Tim 6:11) – certain carnal, sinful practices – to run away from them, not just to lift up the blind and let the sunlight in, but flee! Take to our feet, do something, get away from it! It tells us to put off one thing and to put on another. Paul exhorts the Corinthians like this: 'Let us cleanse ourselves from all filthiness of the flesh and spirit' (2 Cor 7:1). And notice, too, the series of commandments and instructions and exhortations, which we find in the fourth and fifth chapters of Paul's letter to the Ephesians. Now these passages do not teach that you and I just surrender ourselves, and do nothing but look to God in faith. Not at all! We are exhorted to do these things and to work out our own salvation along those various lines.

Furthermore, it is surely right to ask what the point and purpose is of all the arguments of the New Testament epistles, if you and I have to do nothing but just surrender and maintain what is called 'the faith position'. Why all these theological arguments at the beginning of every epistle? Why are these early Christians reminded of their status, and of this great doctrine? For this reason: the New Testament authors always go on to say, Therefore, in the light of all this truth, apply it! Put it into practice! Every one of the New Testament epistles is divided into two sections – doctrine and the application of the doctrine. Paul, for example, puts it so perfectly in Romans 6:1, 'What shall we say *then*? Shall we continue in sin …?' and he goes on to apply the great truths of the earlier chapters. So we must look at it like this: God works in us fundamentally by producing in us a new nature, and disposition. He creates within us new desires and longings after holiness and sanctification and the godly life. Indeed he creates within us the will and the power to live such a life, but he does it all through the word. Nor does he leave us, as it were, doing nothing. He acts upon us so as to produce in us a mighty activity of our own.

Perhaps I can put it best with another negative. God does not do this work in us directly, but indirectly, through the truth. This is a vital principle. So many people think that because we say that this is fundamentally God's work then it is, as it were, something that God does immediately and directly upon our souls and we just have to accept what he does, we just have to 'let go and let God' do these things to us. But that is a false understanding of the teaching of Scripture especially at this point. In our Lord's own words, he does not do the work immediately but mediately through his word, which is the truth. And so he does not teach us to surrender ourselves and every sin to him, and then trust him to deliver us out of those sins, or to take those sins out of us. Some teach that all we have to do, having told God that we want to be delivered, is to believe he has done it, and then we shall eventually find that it has happened. But I do not understand the teaching of Scripture in that way. I do not know of a single scripture – and I speak advisedly – which tells me to take my sin, the particular thing that gets me down, to God in prayer and ask him to deliver me from it and then trust in faith that he will.

Now that teaching is also often put like this: you must say to a man who is constantly defeated by a particular sin, 'I think your only hope is to take it to Christ and Christ will take it from you.' But what does Scripture say in Ephesians 4:28 to the man who finds himself constantly guilty of stealing, to a man who sees something he likes and takes it? What am I to tell such a man? Am I to say, 'Take that sin to Christ and ask him to deliver you?' No, what the apostle Paul tells him is this: 'Let him that stole, steal no more.' Just that. Stop doing it. And if it is fornication or adultery or lustful thoughts, again: Stop doing it, says Paul. He does not say, 'Go and pray to Christ to deliver you.' No. You stop doing that, he says, as becomes children of God. My friends, we have become unscriptural. If you want further evidence, lest somebody thinks it is only the teaching of Paul, let me come to the teaching of the apostle Peter, which is exactly the same; it is the whole teaching of Scripture, which we seem to have forgotten. We read in 1 Peter 1:14 and 15, 'As obedient children, not fashioning yourselves according to the former lusts in your ignorance: but as he which hath called you is holy so be ye holy in all manner of conversation.' It is something that *you* have to do. You must turn your back on these things because you are a child of God. Peter puts it still more strongly, in a sense, in 1 Peter 4:1-4: 'Forasmuch then as Christ has suffered for us in the flesh, arm yourselves likewise with the same mind: for he that hath suffered in the flesh hath ceased from sin; that he no longer should live the rest of his time in the flesh to the lusts of men, but to the will of God' – then listen to the argument – 'For the time past of our life may suffice us to have wrought the will of the Gentiles, when we walked in lasciviousness, lusts, excess of wine, revellings, banquetings, and abominable idolatries: wherein they think it strange that ye run not with them to the same excess of riot, speaking evil of you.'

You must not do it, says Peter. He does not say Surrender it to Christ and ask him to deliver you from it; what he says is, Realise who you are and stop doing it. That is the teaching of Scripture: it tells us that if we really are what we claim to be, then we must stop sinning and we must purify ourselves. It reminds us that God has saved us in Christ, and has put the Holy Spirit into us, and that we already have the power within us, in the Holy Spirit. What we must learn to do is not to grieve the Spirit, but to yield to his promptings and to the strength and power that he gives us. It is we who are exhorted to do these things; God does not do this work in us directly but indirectly.

Not only that, surely we must agree that if the other teaching is right and all I have to do with the sin that gets me down is to take it to Christ, then why should I not do it with all sins? This would mean that I become perfect and sinless – it is the teaching of sinless perfection. The people who hold that teaching would claim that they do not believe in sinless perfection, yet that is the logical conclusion of their teaching. No, that is not biblical doctrine. Rather, the Bible teaches that God does this work in us indirectly through the truth, by the word, by the teaching, by the enlightening, by the under-standing, all of which is worked in us by the power of the Holy Spirit. And thus when we come to consider together the various Scriptures and their teaching with regard to this all-important matter, I think we shall see that the argument of the Bible everywhere is perfectly consistent with itself. God does this work in us by reminding us of who we are. He does it by warnings, and by making us realise the truth concerning himself; and the final argument is that 'every man that hath this hope in him purifieth himself, even as he is pure' (1 Jn 3:3).

We have not finished with this yet. There are other propositions I must put to you; there are other negatives that I must of necessity emphasise before we come to look positively at the great and glorious and transcendant truth which God uses in order to sanctify his people.

# 5

## Sanctification – a Continuous Process

*Sanctify them through thy truth: thy word is truth (v. 17).*

We are still considering, let me remind you, the doctrine of sanctification, which is inevitably brought to our attention by this particular petition here in our Lord's last great high priestly prayer. Our Lord, you remember, is offering certain petitions for those men he is leaving in the world and for all who are going to believe on their word. The first petition is that they may be kept from the evil one, and then follows this petition that God should sanctify them, and sanctify them in and through the truth. We have seen that he prays that because this is the grand end and object of salvation, not merely that we may be forgiven but that we may be sanctified, that we may become entirely devoted to God and fit to spend eternity in his glorious presence. And we have looked together at the way in which our Lord tells us that he sanctifies himself because he must ultimately face death on the cross and all its shame and suffering in order that we might thus be sanctified.

Then we came on to consider the method of sanctification and we began our consideration of that in the last study. It was not a complete consideration, there were many things which we did not deal with, and now as we continue with it I would ask you to be patient and realise that it is a great and vast subject which cannot be dealt with in one short study. Incidentally, may I comment in passing that if a man can present his doctrine

57

of sanctification in one brief study, then I suggest that there is
something wrong with his doctrine. Perhaps the main criticism
of many a popular teaching about sanctification is that it can be
so presented in a few minutes. For that, as we shall see, is something very different from the teaching of the New Testament
itself.

So, then, in looking at this doctrine of sanctification we have
seen that certain great principles must at once be laid down in the
light of this particular verse only. We have seen that it is God's
work and that the way in which he does it is in the truth, or
through the truth, and in pointing out that particular aspect we
have laid down certain negatives. The first was that this does not
mean that God does everything for us and that we have nothing
to do. We are exhorted to do things, and we are told that God
is working in us in order that we may work them out.

The second negative was that God does not do this work
directly but indirectly. He does it in and through the truth. This
is a principle, of course, that not only applies to this subject of
sanctification but to many others also. There is a good deal of
interest in faith healing in these days and sometimes some of
these friends seem to fail to realise that there again God works
indirectly as well as directly. The use of means does not mean
absence of faith; these things are not opposites. God does not
always heal us directly—indeed the common practice is for God
to heal us indirectly through the use of men, physicians and sur-
geons, medicaments and operations and various other means. It
is a great fallacy to think that God must always work directly or
he is not working at all. The normal procedure is the indirect
method and I am suggesting that that is so in this matter of
sanctification. He does it through the truth.

And now we must continue with some additional negatives.
I should be very happy if it were unnecessary to introduce these
negatives, but after all teaching is not only meant to be positive.
We are not only to present the truth we are also to warn people
against error, and that is why the negatives are so essential.

That being so, the next negative I would suggest is that
sanctification must never be thought of as an experience but

always as a state and condition, as the work which God does in us, by the Holy Spirit; or, to use the language of Scripture, it is the process whereby we are being 'conformed to the image of his Son'. That is how Paul describes it in Romans 8:29 and that is the right way to conceive of our salvation, that we are being conformed increasingly to the image, to the pattern, of the Son of God. That is the whole object of salvation, to make us more and more like him. Therefore, it is, of necessity, a matter of our condition and not an experience which we may enjoy for a while and then lose. Read again Ephesians 2:10 where Paul says 'for we are his workmanship' – by which he means that we are something that is being made by him, an object which is being fashioned and formed by God, something which he is bringing into being. We are, Paul continues, 'created in Christ Jesus unto good works which God hath before ordained that we should walk in them'. That again makes it quite clear that it is a condition, and not merely an experiential position in which you find yourself from time to time, so that when you lose the experience you revert to where you were at the beginning.

Or, to put it in the language of the apostle Peter, it is a condition in which we are growing 'in grace, and in the knowledge of our Lord and Saviour Jesus Christ' (2 Pet 3:18). We are growing, developing, advancing! The Scripture talks about babes in Christ, and then about young men and old men. All these pictures are suggestive of growth and development, and that, too, implies a condition and state, and not merely an experience. It is, therefore, a very grievous fallacy to think that sanctification is simply an experience in which one is at that moment conscious of elevated and good thoughts and is free of all evil ones.

However, let us be clear about the relationship of this condition to experience. Since it is a condition of sanctification, and of growth in grace, and development in holiness, it obviously involves experience. And we know that in this process, by the grace of God, we do have experiences which are most helpful for our sanctification. An unusual experience of the nearness of God or of the love of God obviously makes us want to hate sin more, and to strive more after holiness; it makes us hunger and thirst after righteousness to a greater degree than before. Experiences are wonderful things, but what I am concerned to emphasise is that they are not sanctification itself. The experience promotes my sanctification and encourages it, and I think that is where the fallacy probably arises, because it is true to say that when we do have these blessed experiences we are aware of being in a better frame than we were before. As a result, people have tended to identify them with sanctification itself, and they are therefore tempted to say that when they are not enjoying that experience then somehow they seem to have lost their sanctification. But they have not, for whatever their experience may be, the work of God in the soul goes on, and thank God that that is so. It is progressive, so while we thank God for subjective experiences and realise their great value and importance in the work of sanctification, we must never rely upon them.

That, then, leads to another negative, which is that we must not therefore think of sanctification as something which is to be received. You may often have heard it put in that form. We are told that as we receive our justification, so also we receive our sanctification; it is presented to us as something which we can accept. But again it seems to me that if we realise that sanctification means the work of God in us, separating us from sin unto himself, then obviously it is something which cannot be received in that way. As we saw earlier, the work of sanctification is something that starts in us from the very first moment of belief. From the moment I realise what sin is and begin to hate it and long to be delivered from it, from that moment, the process of sanctification is going steadily forward. It is progressive, and not complete in this life and world. And, therefore, because of this and because it advances in this way, it is obviously something which I cannot receive in one act.

There is great confusion at this point. People seem to think of sanctification as if it were similar to justification. A man is justified once and for all. It is one concrete experience, a matter of my standing and status. But sanctification, by definition, is this progressive, increasing work that goes on in our souls, bringing us more and more into the image of Jesus Christ. How can that be received as one experience? Surely it is quite impossible!

We can put it like this. If sanctification were a gift that we received from God, then, as we have seen earlier, I think it follows of necessity that we must be believers in a complete sinless perfection. Every gift that God gives is perfect and entire. God never gives a partial gift and if he gives sanctification to a man as a gift, it is complete and perfect. So if I receive sanctification, I must then and there be made perfectly whole and sinless. Then, of course, the question arises, how can I ever sin again? What is there in me that would ever make me responsive to sin? No, it is quite clear that sanctification is not a gift that one can receive as one can receive the gift of justification. It is rather this continuous, steadily advancing work that God does in us, in order that we may work it out with fear and trembling. And again we are reminded of all those exhortations in the New Testament Scriptures to keep free from sinful lusts – 'Let him that stole, steal no more' and so on. All these exhortations make it quite clear that sanctification is not a gift to be received but is a process which God is working out in us.

Let me put it in another way: in the light of all these things we must not think of sanctification as something which happens suddenly. This again is a point which must be emphasised. People seem to think (and here they are logical though they are wrong) that if it is a gift to be received, then obviously it must be something that happens suddenly; you receive a gift, it happens suddenly, and you take possession of the thing offered you. But surely this is quite incompatible with the New Testament teaching on this matter. It is, rather, characteristic of the cults, of a man-made idea of sanctification. We always like to do things suddenly, and to have anything we want, at once. So you find that those teachings always offer a kind of short cut, and that is their appeal to the carnal mind, because we are always so impatient, always in such a desperate hurry. But this very verse which we are now considering makes it quite impossible for sanctification to be something that happens suddenly. 'Sanctify them,' says our Lord, 'in thy truth.'

Our Lord has already said the same thing in John 8:31–32. He said to certain men who appeared to believe: 'If ye continue in my word, then are ye my disciples indeed; and ye shall know the truth, and the truth shall make you free.' It is always the truth, therefore, and that is something which is progressive. We do not grasp the whole of the truth at once, we go through these stages, from babes to full matured age, from being a child to being an old man, as it were, in terms of faith. We see the same thing again in Philippians 2:12, that verse which I am quoting so frequently, 'Work out your own salvation with fear and trembling' – it is something you keep doing – 'not as in my presence only,' says Paul, 'but now much more in my absence.' The exhortation in all these writings is to continue steadfast, to progress and to go on with the work. That is the great appeal that runs right through the New Testament. You have started, do not stop, keep on with it. And surely that is why this process is not something which we must regard as happening suddenly, and it is astonishing that anybody should ever have had such a false idea about it.

Yet people seem to me to be trying to defend this doctrine of suddenly becoming sanctified because they somehow feel it is dishonouring to God not to believe in it. But there, I think, the fallacy emerges. It is the fallacy to which I have already referred, that of thinking that God must always work directly and yet, as I have already shown you, in the matter of physical healing, for example, God's normal way of working is to do it indirectly. All healing comes from God; no healing is possible apart from him and we should always realise that, whether we use means, or whether we stake our dependence upon God alone. You can use the best means in the world, but if it is not God's will that you be healed you will not be, because all healing comes from God.

But it is not only a matter of healing. Look at God's method in nature, for instance; it is always this same indirect method. God's ordained way is that the farmer should plough the earth, then sow the seed, and then roll it over and wait until the harvest comes several months later. Now it would be equally apposite to ask why God does it like that. Why does he not make the crop and the fruit come the very next day after the farmer has put the seed into the ground? He could do it if he wanted to, for with God all things are possible. Why does God make man wait all these months from the time of sowing to the time of harvest? But that is exactly what God does. He has chosen that it shall happen in that way, and as he does this in the growth of things in nature, and in the whole of life, our physical frames and everything else, that also seems to be his method of sanctification. Indeed, as you look at the experience of the saints throughout the centuries that is the thing to which you find them all testifying.

Take another illustration. Why has God allowed Satan to continue in being? Why do we still have to look forward to the day when Satan shall finally be put down and thrown in to the lake of fire and destroyed? Satan was really defeated by the Lord Jesus Christ upon the cross, but that was nearly 2,000 years ago. Some might well ask, Why did God not immediately destroy Satan? But that is God's way. It has pleased him that Satan should be allowed to continue in being, to trouble and to try and to torment God's own people. Or again we might ask, Why did God not destroy death at once? By rising from the dead the Lord Jesus Christ has really conquered death, and yet it is still true to say that the last enemy that shall be conquered and destroyed is death. Christian people are still subject to it and have to die. So why did God not instantly take it right away from us? But he has not done so; death remains as a fact. It has pleased God, I say it once more, to leave us subject to physical death, and thus we go on in this life and in this world. And in the same way you might ask why God does not give every Christian, immediately he becomes a Christian, perfect health, and deliver him from all the things to which the human physical frame is subject in this life and world. He does not do so because his method all along the line is to work this work in a gradual, progressive and increasing manner.

I sometimes think that here again the confusion has arisen because people fail to differentiate between the sudden realisation of certain aspects of truth, and sanctification itself. And I think, too, that the false teaching often arises in this way. You are told the story of a man who undoubtedly has been converted but he has gone on living a kind of humdrum Christian life for a number of years; then suddenly he hears of a teaching which he had never heard of or realised before, and suddenly, from having seen this wonderful thing, his whole life has been changed. He seems to have had a second conversion, some mighty blessing has descended upon him and he is never the same again after that second experience. Ah, they say, what happened to him at that point was that whereas before he was only justified, he has now become sanctified in addition, and it happened suddenly.

Now let us analyse an experience like that. What really happened? Well I think we must all now agree that if that man was truly converted before the second experience, if he really had seen himself as a sinner, if he had come to see that his only hope of salvation is that Christ had died for him and his sins, and if he was trusting to that in order that he might be delivered from sin and the wrath of God, that man's sanctification was already proceeding. As we have seen, you cannot be saved without the process of sanctification already starting. It is impossible to think of justification in isolation. So that the first fallacy is the view that the man was only justified.

Then what of this next experience? Well, clearly what has happened here is that though the man had received and had believed vital Christian truth, his realisation of it was incomplete, and what undoubtedly happened to this man was that he came to the realisation of other aspects of truth that he had not hitherto understood. In grasping this, perhaps the possibility came to him of a more sanctified condition, of a further advance and growth in grace and knowledge. He came to that realisation suddenly and therefore he, as it were, made a great spurt forward in his sanctification. But what really happened to that man was not that he was receiving sanctification for the first time, but that there was a visible development and advance in the process of sanctification in him.

This, again, is a phenomenon with which we are familiar in

many other realms. It happens to us with regard to secular knowledge. How often have you been struggling with a problem for a very long time and then suddenly you see it, and it is solved? That does not mean that all the struggling that had gone before was useless. Take any one of these great inventions, or take the advance in the realm of science, or the application of science to life, and you will invariably find that there has been a great background of work leading up to the final discovery. It would seem suddenly to have sprung from nowhere to absolute knowledge but only because we have not understood all that has really happened. In spiritual things we realise certain things perhaps suddenly or perhaps gradually; the realisation may be sudden, but that is not the sanctification. Rather, the realisation of some truth leads to the application of that truth and the application of that truth may cause a sudden jump forward, a sudden advance in this process of sanctification.

These sudden realisations of truth are therefore most valuable and helpful. Let me use a simple, homely illustration. Have you not often noticed in the spring that when the farmer has sown the seed, but the weather has been bad, nothing seems to happen – perhaps you can barely see that the seed has germinated and it is only just beginning to show above the ground. Then you get a shower and, following the shower, a burst of warm sunshine. You go out and look at that same field the next morning and you are astonished. Everything seems to have happened in the night. It looks as if all was due to the shower and the sunshine. Suddenly there seems to have been growth and you say to yourself, 'There was nothing yesterday, but look at it now.' But what has really happened? Again, of course, the truth is that the process has been going on for weeks. The shower and the sudden burst of sunshine have made it all leap forward, but the leaping forward is not the beginning of the process, it is but the advancing of it. As you go on you may find that phenomenon repeated many times: another shower, another burst of sunshine, another leap. But the process is one, and continuous; it is progressive and always developing.

And surely it is exactly like that in this whole question of sanctification. I am sure that any Christian looking back across life can testify to the same thing. You can see certain landmarks, certain special periods, certain times when things seemed unusually clear and you seemed to make an advance. Then there seemed to be times when things remained dormant and nothing happened, until, again, something happened. That is the process of sanctification. It is not sudden. The experience and the realisation may be, but the thing itself is progressive.

This brings me to my last negative, which is that we must never think of sanctification as something which happens without a struggle and fight. Here again, of course, we realise that there is a teaching which would emphasise that sanctification is effortless. But I think it follows from the teaching that we have been laying down, that that cannot be the case. Once more, the view that we are delivered from all struggling and strain and fighting is characteristic of the cults and false human teaching. That is why they always tend to appeal to us, because they offer us something easy. But as you look at the teaching of Scripture, I suggest that you do not find anything like that, and I am not only referring to the fight that is outside us, but also to the enemy that is still within us. The Scripture tells us that the remnants of the old man are still here – you do not get rid of him – and as long as that is the case, there will be a fight and a struggle. Scriptural teaching about the flesh involves the necessity of a struggle: 'The flesh lusteth against the Spirit, and the Spirit against the flesh' (Gal 5:17).

'Ah yes,' says someone, 'but that is before you receive the blessing of sanctification.' Wait a minute! Let us be quite honest. Do you know anybody who would tell you that he or she has been entirely delivered from the flesh? Is there no struggle within you? How easy it is to put a theoretical position – is it true in practice? The flesh is allowed to remain just as death is allowed. God does not deliver us from this. He puts in the new man, who can overcome the flesh and the old man, and the old nature, but the remnants of the old nature and the flesh are still there and that means struggle, that means fight. That is why we are exhorted not to grieve the Holy Spirit, not to quench the

Holy Spirit; that is why we are exhorted to mortify our members that are on the earth; that is why we are told to mortify the flesh and the deeds of the body. We are told to watch, to purify ourselves and to cleanse ourselves, and we are told to fight the good fight of faith. All these exhortations arise, of necessity, because of this struggle that is in life.

We must not, however, forget what I have laid down as my first principle, which is that we are not left to engage in this struggle alone. The work of God has been started in us. If you are a Christian at all, the Holy Spirit is in you, and the Holy Spirit gives you the power to fight. But you have to do the fighting, you have to put off the old man and put on the new – that is scriptural teaching and it involves a struggle. But it is not a hopeless fight, because I am certain of the ultimate victory.

As we saw in our last study, if this is not true, then I simply cannot understand a single New Testament epistle, and I do not see why the New Testament was ever written. But these letters were written because these men, whom God appointed as pastors and teachers, knew that the Christians needed to be exhorted continually to go on with the fight and the struggle, for if they did not they were defeated. Therefore we, too, must fight, we must struggle and we must work out our own salvation, not with light-hearted joviality, but with fear and trembling, because it is God that worketh in us, both to will and to do of his good pleasure.

So that brings us to the end of the negatives, all of which have been necessary, not because of the biblical teaching, but because of other false teachings. But having thus dealt with the negatives, we are now free to continue with a consideration of the positive teaching of the Scriptures, which is, 'Sanctify them through thy truth.' We shall look at this blessed, wonderful, large, comprehensive truth of God, this full-orbed gospel that does not separate justification from sanctification, but says that it is all a work of God. We shall consider a great truth that cannot be divided up into separate movements, a movement for evangelism, a movement for sanctification, a movement about the Second Coming, a movement about this and that. No, for the truth is one and it must not be atomised in this way; it is unscriptural and dangerous to do so. We are looking at this great truth in all its wondrous fullness, we see how each aspect of it fits into the whole, and we see the hand of God in it all. We see how he starts the work in the babe, and continues it until eventually we shall all arrive complete and perfect, even into 'the measure of the stature of the fullness of Christ' himself.

May God give us grace to do so and may we all realise that this is not a theoretical matter, but that this is the thing for which Christ died, the thing for which he sanctified himself, namely, that we may be sanctified and might be made meet and fit to dwell face to face with God in glory and to enjoy him for ever and ever.

# 6

## One All-inclusive Truth

*Sanctify them through thy truth: thy word is truth (v. 17).*

In our last two studies, we have been looking at God's method of
sanctifying us. We laid down the negatives and warned about
certain dangers, and so now we are in a position to approach the
truth positively. The great statement, as we have seen, is that *the
work of sanctification in us is done by God through the medium
of the truth*. If we say that our sanctification takes place by God
bringing us into the realm of the truth, in order that the truth may
act upon us, then the vital question for us is, therefore, What is
this truth which God uses in order to promote our sanctification?

Here again there is more than one view. There are those –
and this is the teaching which I think needs to be coun-
teracted first of all – who seem to regard the truth to which
our Lord refers here as just being some wonderful, special
teaching which they go on repeating. But that, surely, is
quite a false understanding of what our Lord means by the
truth. Indeed, our Lord here, at once realising the danger, it
seems to me, safeguards us against it by defining the truth:
'Sanctify them through thy truth, thy word is truth.' What,
then, is this word? The answer can be found in this chapter
in verses 6, 7, 8, which we have already considered.[1] It is not
some peculiar teaching about sanctification which a man goes

---

[1] In Volume 2, *Safe in the World* (Crossway Books, 1988)

on to after justification. No, it is the holy word. Our Lord says, 'I have manifested thy name unto the men which thou gavest me out of the world: thine they were, and thou gavest them me; and they have kept thy word. Now they have known that all things whatsoever thou hast given me are of thee. For I have given unto them the words which thou gavest me; and they have received them, and have known surely that I came out from thee, and they have believed that thou didst send me.' 'Thy word is truth,' he says here in verse 17 – and that is the truth.

So our Lord is teaching us that God sanctifies us through the truth, by means of the truth and in the truth. He is referring partly to his own teaching – the truth by which we are sanctified is not only what we read in Romans, chapters 6, 7 and 8, it is all the teaching of the Gospels, this word which God had given to the Son, and which the Son taught his followers. It is not just one section of the truth, it is the whole of the truth. Everything he teaches in the Sermon on the Mount, and everything he teaches elsewhere, all that is what God uses in order to bring about our sanctification.

But, of course, it does not only include that. In John 14, 15 and 16 our Lord has just told these disciples that the Holy Spirit, when he comes and is given to them in fullness, will teach them and lead them into all truth; it is still the same idea. Our Lord describes him as the Spirit of truth: not simply as the true Spirit as against the false spirits, but in a very special way as the Spirit through whom the truth of God comes to men and women and is mediated to them. Our Lord says, 'I have yet many things to say unto you, but ye cannot bear them now. Howbeit when he, the Spirit of truth, is come, he will guide you into all truth' (John 16:12 – 13). And, of course, when the Holy Spirit came he did enlighten these apostles, and we have their teaching recorded for us in these various New Testament epistles. So we see that the truth that God uses in order to bring about our sanctification is all the truth we have in the Gospels, together with all the truth that we have in the New Testament epistles. All the demonstration and doctrine, all the exhortation and appeals, the whole of he New Testament, is the truth which he has used in order to ɔring about our sanctification. So that is our basic definition; the ruth about sanctification, and the truth which leads to it, is not ɔome isolated department on its own to which you go, having ɔeen somewhere else first. The whole of the truth about the person of our Lord is this word of God which leads to our sanctification.

Because of this, then, we must now consider this truth, because without it sanctification is not possible. We saw in our negatives that sanctification does not take place as the result of God acting directly upon us. No, he does it through showing this particular truth. So if we are anxious that we should grow in grace and in the knowledge of the Lord and that we should conform more and more to the image of God's dear Son; if it is our supreme ambition to know him and to be devoted to him, then the first thing we must do is to pay attention to this truth.

Now it is a truth which is divided up in the Scriptures into many aspects, but before we come to look at them in detail, or in terms of these different facets, it is important that we should begin by looking at it as a whole. To do this, therefore, we must stand back and look at the great New Testament message which promotes sanctification, and realise that there are certain major principles with respect to it. Most people get into trouble in the Christian life, and in almost every profession, because they rush to details before they grasp the principles. In order truly to understand any science or any branch of knowledge, we must start with great fundamental principles, and it is only as we have them firmly in our minds that we can go on to details, because if we have not grasped the principles, the details will not help us. Most heresies have arisen because men have fastened on details in that way.

So, then, here are some of these principles which I would put for your consideration, and which seem to stand out on the surface of this New Testament truth, this word of God. The first is that we again see the importance of not regarding sanctification primarily from the standpoint of an experience. Sanctification is primarily the application of the truth to ourselves, it is not first and foremost having or receiving an experience. Rather, what happens in sanctification is that God takes this truth, this word of his, and by the Holy Spirit brings it to us, opens our understanding of it and enables us to apprehend it. So that after we have received the truth and apprehended it, we then proceed to apply it to ourselves. And the whole time God is enabling us to do that.

I emphasise this first great principle because I would not hesitate to assert that perhaps the main trouble which most of us have in this matter of sanctification is that we tend to be waiting for some experience instead of taking the truth, applying our minds to it, and then applying it entirely to our lives. We seem to think that what happens is that somehow we are put into a sanctified position and that once we get there, everything is going to be all right. But it never seems to happen – we are still waiting for some experience. That is not the New Testament teaching at all. What the New Testament says is that we must realise the truth about God, the truth about ourselves, the truth about what Christ has done for us and about our standing and status.

That is why Paul offered that prayer for the church at Ephesus. What you need, he says, is that 'the eyes of your understanding' may be enlightened (Eph 1:18), because if you only knew the truth, then your position would be changed. So we must not wait for the experience and say that then everything will be all right. No, the way to come to an experience is rather in dependence upon the Holy Spirit who is at work within us, to approach the truth, to study, to understand and to grasp it and then to apply it to ourselves. Now that is surely the argument of all the New Testament epistles. Why were they ever written? Why was not just a brief note sent to all those Christian people saying, 'All you have to do is to wait for an experience of sanctification'? No, these people had received the Holy Spirit, so what they were constantly being told was that they must grasp the truth that had been given to them, live by it, and apply it to themselves. That will become clearer as we come on to certain other things.

I would put my second principle like this: our main and basic need in sanctification is not power but light and knowledge and instruction. Now I put it in that form deliberately. I think it is true to say that we all tend to feel that our basic need is the need of power – we want power in our lives; we feel that we know what is right, and we want to do it, but we somehow lack the power to do it, and we long to be charged with this power, which will enable us to live aright. 'Sanctify them,' says our Lord in his petition, but it is 'sanctify them *in thy truth, thy word is truth.*' Fill them with knowledge, he says, give them the understanding, apply the truth to them.

There is no question at all but that the devil encourages us to think that our need in sanctification is power, because the devil's object is to keep us in ignorance. He first of all keeps the whole world in ignorance about its condition and its relationship to God. He blinds the eyes and the minds of them that believe not, he blinds their minds to the truth about God and about them-selves and about righteousness and about judgement. He tries to keep us out of the entire realm of the Christian faith, but if in spite of his efforts we become Christians, he still continues with his work and he now tries to blind us to the real truth about our-selves as it is in Christ Jesus.

I suggest that as long as we are in this life, there is a sense in which even Christian people will always have to fight the battle of justification by faith only. As Paul pointed out to the Gala-tians, the danger is that having started in the Spirit we continue in the flesh, and we are all constantly faced with this danger. It is always the work of the devil, and he does it in a particular way in connection with this whole question of sanctification. We think that what we need is power, so that we have nothing to do but wait till the power comes, whereas the teaching is that what we need is to know this truth, the truth about ourselves in our relationship to God – 'The eyes of your understanding being enlightened that ye may know what is the hope of his calling, and what the riches of the glory of his inheritance in the saints and what is the exceeding greatness of his power to us-ward who believe' (Eph 1:18–19).

For as Christian people the power is already in us. You canno[t] be a Christian without having received the Holy Spirit. 'N[o] man can say that Jesus is the Lord, but by the Holy Ghost' (1 Co[r] 12:3). We are not Christians unless we have received the Hol[y] Spirit, it is a part of our regeneration and rebirth; the gift of th[e] Spirit is the possession of every truly converted Christia[n] believer. Therefore, the power to live the Christian life i[s] already there. So what we really need is to know the truth abou[t] ourselves as Christians; we need to know that we are childre[n] of God, that our sins have been forgiven, that we are reconcile[d] to God, and that we need have no worry about that. We nee[d] to see ourselves 'seated in the heavenly places in Christ Jesus'. We need to know that the very hairs of our head are all numbered, that we are thus special people in the sight of God and we need to know about the blessed hope that is awaiting us. That is the teaching of the New Testament. For our real trouble is that we tend to have our own ideas as to what a Christian is, instead of accepting the New Testament definition.

I am most anxious to emphasise this, because there is nothing which is so blessed and so releasing as to be taken out of that subjectivity that is always looking at itself, and, rather, to see one's self as one truly is in the purpose of God, as it is outlined in the New Testament. The trouble is that we tend to go to the word with these prejudices of ours, and we do not really take in what we are reading; we do not allow it to speak to us. We fail to realise that this description of the New Testament man should be a description of *us*, not only of the first Christians, nor of some ideal person, but a description of every one of us if we are Christians. Thus the vital thing is to realise what we are and if we realise that, then we should begin to realise 'the power that worketh in us' (Eph 3:20).

So my third proposition is that most of our troubles in this matter are ultimately in the realm of the will. Now I want to put this carefully. Here again I say that we tend to fool ourselves and to think that our wills are all right, but that what we need is the power to carry out the will. Once more we are deluded by the devil at that point. People often tend to put it like this: 'You know, I have tried and tried for years to get rid of this thing out of my life, and I pray to God about it.' We need to pause between the two parts of that statement, because it generally happens in this way. They first of all try to get rid of their problem themselves. Then they go to somebody who seems to be an expert in these matters, and he says, 'Ah yes, but of course that is exactly where you have gone wrong. You have been trying to do it yourself, and you never will. You must give up trying and you must pray about it – stop your own efforts and just pray to God about it, and ask him to take it from you, and it will go.' Then they tell you that they have prayed about it, and they have gone to meetings, and heard other people say that their sins have suddenly been taken away, but they themselves are still burdened, and they do not know what to do next. They feel that they are failures and they are desperate.

It seems to me that there is only one real trouble with such people and it is entirely in the realm of the will. Otherwise they are either saying that God does not want to deliver them, or that he cannot deliver them. That is their position. They have tried the proposed remedy, they have tried to surrender themselves utterly and they have asked God to take this burden from them, but they say that they still have it.

But that is where the trouble arises, and I feel that there is only one thing to do at this point, and that is to be brutal, and to say to these friends, 'The real trouble with you is that you have a divided will. You are saying, in effect, either that God does not want to take this thing away, or that he cannot. But the trouble is that you do not really want to get rid of it; you are fond of it. You are not hungering and thirsting after righteousness, you are really unhappy in your mind. You know it is wrong but you like it – that is the trouble. It is as we read in John 3:19 "Men loved darkness rather than light."'

The only thing to do with such people is to bring them face to face with truth, and to confront them with the fact that if they claim to be Christians, they are really saying a number of things about themselves. If they claim to believe in God, and in the Holy Spirit, how can they go on with this particular thing, whatever it may be? You have to convince their wills about this matter, you have to put their will right.

Then the fourth proposition is this: the will, as I understand this New Testament teaching, is never to be coerced or forced into a decision. Now that must be said, even in the light of what we have just been suggesting. I still say the sort of people I have been describing, you have to be brutal and show them that their trouble is in the realm of the will, but it is very important that you do not force the will, or get them to do so. You must show them the truth, in order that their wills may be persuaded by the truth. Let me put this practically. So often you find that what happens with such people is that pressure is put upon them – 'You must decide it here and now,' they are urged; their will is forced, and then they are told they have promised and that they must never go back on their word.

But people who have done that often find themselves later on in the position that the only thing that really holds them there is their own decision or their own view. Now that may be quite a good thing in a practical sense – it is certainly extremely good psychology, – but it is utterly bad New Testament teaching, if indeed it is New Testament teaching at all. This is because you and I must be held to the New Testament position not by our pledges, but by the truth. We must realise, therefore, that the will is to be persuaded by the truth, and that that is how God works. He never forces our will, but rather presents the truth to us in such a way that we want it – 'Every man that hath this hope in him purifieth himself, even as he is pure' (1 Jn 3:3). So what the New Testament does is hold the blessed hope before us, and then, having seen it for ourselves, we say, 'If I am going there, I cannot behave like this here and now; I am jeopardising my own liberty.' The truth has come to us, and as we see the truth we want to be delivered from sin, and to belong to God.

Let me put it quite plainly. I cannot see, from New Testament teaching, that there is the slightest justification for ever calling upon people in a meeting to decide to go in for sanctification and for bringing pressure upon them to do so by forcing them to a decision. If that procedure is wrong in evangelism, it is equally wrong in this matter of sanctification. A man's will must never be approached directly, because the will must always be approached through the truth. The truth should be presented to the will in such a way that the will desires it, needs and accepts it. This it does freely and without any sense of constraint, and puts into practice what it has willed. Therefore, if you are ever confronted by a man who tells you that he is defeated, and that he is a slave to, or a victim of, something, the thing to do is to remind him of the whole nature of the truth. You do not spend your time discussing the particular problem. Rather, you say, 'Are you a child of God?' You address him in terms of the truth, and so the will, the whole time, is being influenced by the truth which is being presented.

Let me put that in the form of another proposition. According to this truth, this word of God in the New Testament, sanctification is not just a matter of being delivered from particular sins. So often you will find that that is what is taught. People seem to think that if only they could get rid of this one sin, they would be sanctified; and it becomes still worse when the entire doctrine is focussed upon deliverance from one particular sin. No, sanctification is a matter of being rightly related to God, and becoming entirely devoted to him. Sanctification means becoming positively holy. It does not just mean I am not guilty of certain sins, because the moment you begin to think of it negatively like that, you are satisfied that you are sanctified; but you may be as far from sanctification, if not further, than the man who is guilty of one or other of those sins, because now you are now guilty of smugness! Sanctification means being devoted to God, not only separated from the world but separated unto God and sharing his life – it is positive holiness.

I proceed, then, to my next principle, the sixth, which is that the New Testament method of dealing with particular sins is never to concentrate upon the particular sin as such, but to bring it into the light and the context of the whole Christian position. I cannot emphasise that principle too strongly. Speaking out of pastoral experience, I have found in practice, that that particular principle is probably the most important of all. May I give you one illustration. I remember a lady once, some twenty years ago, coming to tell me of a crippling problem in her Christian spiritual life. She told me that she had a terrible horror and dread of thunderstorms. Apparently she had once been in a bad thunderstorm, and it had looked as if she might be killed. Ever since then the fear of thunder and lightning had gripped her, and it had come to such a pass that if she was going to a place of worship and happened to see a large cloud, she would begin to say to herself, 'A thunderstorm is coming! So there would be a terrible conflict within her and it usually ended in her turning back and going home. It seemed to her that the one problem of her life was this fear and dread of thunderstorms. She told me she had struggled with this problem and done her best to get rid of it. She had been to consult many Christian people about it and they all told her to pray about it, and to ask God to deliver her from it. She had been praying for this for twenty-two years, but it was worse rather than better, and she went on to tell me how she longed to be delivered from this one thing which was marring her Christian life.

Now it seemed to me that the one thing to say to that woman was this – and it came as a shock to her – 'Stop praying about this particular fear, for while you are praying, you are reminding yourself of it. You must stop thinking about yourself in terms of fear. Never think about thunderstorms; turn your back upon that altogether. What you must do is to think about yourself as a disciple of the Lord Jesus Christ and as one who belongs to him. You are known as a Christian, therefore you are claiming certain things. You must concentrate upon positive Christianity, not upon a negative fear of one sin.' And after much instruction she saw it and the fear of thunderstorms was forgotten. It did not happen suddenly, but as she concentrated on the Christian life, the fear just went.

Often people come and talk about one particular sin. They have been concentrating upon that one sin as though the whole Christian life is in just that one sin. But I adopt the word of Paul in Romans: 'The kingdom of God is not meat and drink' (Rom 14:17). There were people in the church who seemed to say that

Christianity was one particular thing: What should you eat and drink? Which day should you observe? But that is not the Christian life! So when a man comes and talks to me about one thing, I talk to him about peace and joy in the Holy Spirit, all these positive elements, and I tell him, 'You must be stretching out after them, and if you do so you will be delivered from the one sin.' That is the New Testament method; it brings the truth to us and gives us this glorious picture of the new man in Christ Jesus.

The next principle is that sanctification must never be thought of as an end in itself but rather as a means to an end. Here again is a very important principle. Our eyes should not be only upon the cultivation of a holy life and freedom from sins. I go further: it should not even be our ambition to be holy men and women. I remember a man saying to me, 'You know, my greatest ambition is to be a holy man.' I said to him, 'Yes, that is the trouble with you!' The goal, I say, is not even to be holy men, nor to attain holiness, but rather to live in fellowship with God. Our goal is the knowledge and the love of God and of his Son Jesus Christ. The goal is not that I should be sanctified, but that I should be walking with him in fellowship and communion, in the light of the knowledge that I am going to spend my eternity with him.

This is the main problem during every season of Lent.[1] The Catholic conception of holiness and mysticism, it seems to me, goes wrong at this very point, for it always concentrate upon the holy condition of the believer. If you read any manual on the holy or devoted life ever written by a Catholic or a mystic, you will usually find that you are exposing yourself to that particular danger. They concentrate attention upon the experimental condition, upon the experience, and then, of course, they take you through the different stages – the stage of torment, the stage of the dark night of the soul – until you ultimately arrive at the stage of holy contemplation.

I remember a man once, an old minister of the gospel, telling

---

[1] This sermon was preached during Lent in 1953.

me that he was struggling, and in a sense really living in order to pass through the experience of the dark night of the soul, because he felt that he had never gone through it. Poor man! It was all subjective; he was simply concerned to be a holy man. But that is where the error comes in. Is it not exactly the same with this observance of Lent? To observe Lent for a certain number of weeks during the year is just to concentrate upon your experience. It is to look at yourself and try to make yourself better, to pull yourself up to a higher level. And, incidentally, what I am saying is not only true of the Catholic form of sanctification and holiness, you will find it coming out in evangelical piety too. The man who is anxious to think of himself as pious, falls into the same error.

But the whole biblical emphasis is not upon that at all, for the New Testament truth, the word of God, always puts it in terms of our personal relationship to the Father and to his Son, Jesus Christ, through the Holy Spirit. In other words, let us forget about our state and condition. Instead, the one question I need to ask myself is this: 'Do I know God? Is Jesus Christ real to me?' Not, 'Am I now no longer full of the sin of which I used to be guilty?' Not, 'Am I observing certain rules and regulations?' It is not, 'Do I spend so much time in reading and prayer?' No, rather, it is this: 'Am I having fellowship with him?' If you do not know this living experience of God, all your negative righteousness is of no value to you.

And that brings me to my last principle which arises out of all that I have been saying, and it is this: the truth about which our Lord speaks is a great truth, a large and comprehensive truth. You can read certain books and listen to certain addresses and you get the impression that the truth which leads to sanctification is really a very simple truth, just one little message – all you have to do is to surrender and wait and keep looking. But this truth about which our Lord speaks is the whole Christian truth! It includes all the epistles, all the Sermon on the Mount and the teaching of the Gospels. It is the whole Bible; it is everything that tells us anything about God.

We hear complaints sometimes that certain types of teaching about sanctification seem to be running to seed, that they seem to be lacking body. It is not surprising, since if you nail the truth down, you cannot get any other result. No, the truth which is concerned about sanctification is not only found in Romans, 6, 7 and 8 – though you are sometimes given the impression that it is there, and nowhere else – it is everywhere. It is all the truth, it is this vast body of doctrine; it is the whole Christian message. That is why I would reiterate that an evangelistic meeting should include sanctification, if it is truly evangelistic. If a Christian can sit back and feel that the message has nothing to say to him, then there has been something wrong with the evangelistic message, for it is one which tells about the holiness of God, and immediately the process of sanctification is going on as it describes the heinousness of sin and as it tells about Christ dying on the cross. Indeed, I can never look at the cross without that truth prompting my sanctification. It is tragic to think that we have divided these things into departments, and separated them from one another. No message whatsoever about the cross is isolated from sanctification; sanctification is involved in every iota of the truth, in all the knowledge of God and our relationship to him, whether it tells about the Eternal Council before the creation of the world, whether it tells about being foreordained and elected, or whether it tells about principalities and powers and a blessed hope. It is all the truth that works upon me by the Holy Spirit, and leads to and promotes my sanctification. 'Sanctify them through thy truth, thy word is truth': every word of God is a word used in our sanctification. 'O the depth of the riches both of the wisdom and knowledge of God!' That is it! We are facing this never ebbing sea, this ocean of God's eternal truth, and to be sanctified means an increasing apprehension of it and an increasing application of it in our daily life.

# 7

# *The Truth about God*

*Sanctify them through the truth: thy word is truth (v. 17).*

We have been emphasising the point that the truth, this word of God which is the truth that sanctifies, is large and great and comprehensive, and that it is wrong to regard it just as one section of biblical teaching, and to say that you have now come to the truth of sanctification, as if that is divorced from every other aspect of truth. Our emphasis is that it is the whole of the truth, every aspect of the truth, that ultimately is used of God by the Holy Spirit in our sanctification.

But obviously, though we hold to that, it is yet a truth which we can sub-divide in an intellectual manner, under certain main headings; Scripture itself does that, and it is right that we should do so also. God condescends to our weakness, and he knows that it is easier for us to receive truth, and to remember it, and to retain it, if it is presented to us under certain groupings or headings. And so it has always been the custom in the church to divide up this one great comprehensive truth, the word of God which sanctifies, under various headings. But again I emphasise that they are nothing but headings; they are not distinct truths which can be isolated and separated from other truths. They are simple sub-divisions in the one all-inclusive comprehensive truth. And it seems to me that we are not presenting the doctrine of sanctification truly unless we at least glance at some of these main headings of the truth which sanctifies.

82

Clearly we cannot go into any one of them exhaustively at his point. The object is rather that we may make sure that certain key principles are emphasised; and as we come to do this, we shall see that there can be no doubt or question at all as to which comes first. I wonder what your answer would be if I put that question: What should be the first heading when you come to consider in detail the truth which sanctifies? What is the first thing you want to emphasise? This is very important, and surely the heading which, without a doubt, should occupy the first position is the truth about God himself.

I wonder whether we would all have started with that? I want to emphasise it because I think we must all plead guilty to the fact that there is a tendency and a danger among us (I am referring now to Christian people, who think from the evangelical standpoint with regard to truth) – though I say it with fear and trembling – to take God for granted. I mean by that, to assume God, to imagine that because we are Christians, and evangelical Christians in particular, then we do not need to consider constantly the truth about God himself. 'That is a truth,' we say, 'that the unconverted need, of course, because they do not think of God; God is not in all their thoughts or in their mind; they are living a godless life.' We know that we need to preach the truth about God himself to the unconverted, but we think that people who are Christians are obviously believers in God, and that therefore there is no need to preach to them and to present constantly the doctrine about God himself.

I wonder what the result would be if we made a careful examination of large numbers of addresses and sermons on this question of sanctification? I wonder how often we would find that the doctrine concerning God himself has been preached on such occasions? I think we would find the answer illuminating. The tendency, the danger is, as we have seen, that we start with the idea that sanctification is just one department only of salvation. We forget that the first beginning of sanctification is the doctrine of God himself.

Let me illustrate this, remembering always that it is a matter which we must approach carefully. Is it not true to say that among certain Christian people there is a tendency to pray to the Lord Jesus Christ rather than to God the Father? Do not misunderstand me. I am not saying that it is wrong to pray to the three persons of the blessed Trinity separately, for there is evidence in the Scriptures that that is the right thing to do. You will find, incidentally, a much greater tendency to do that in the hymns. There is much more individual prayer to the three persons separately in our hymn-books than there is in the Scriptures. Yet surely no one can dispute the point that in the Scripture itself prayer is generally addressed to God in the name of Christ, through and by the Holy Spirit. We cannot come to God except by the blood of Jesus. We ask everything in Christ's name and for Christ's sake. But the prayer is ultimately addressed to God the Father. I am simply indicating that there is an increasing tendency for people to pray to the Lord Jesus Christ and it is entirely due to the same reason, it is just another indication of the way in which, because our doctrine is not based four-square upon the teaching of the Scripture itself, we have departmentalised it and somehow or other (it is a terrible thing to say) we tend to forget God. I am emphasising, therefore, the fact that the Bible itself always starts with God in every respect. God is at the beginning, and he continues right through. It is a book about God. It is all about him, and everything in it is designed simply to bring us to him. Thus, not to remind ourselves that the doctrine concerning God is central, and always covers and overrules everything else, is, it seems to me, to fall into very grievous error, for if we are wrong at this point it is certain we shall be wrong everywhere else.

Indeed, is it not the case that in this matter of sanctification our tendency is always to start with ourselves, instead of starting with God? I have got this sin that is worrying me and always getting me down, this sin that defeats me, and my tendency is to say, 'What can be done about this sin, this problem of mine? How can I get rid of this thing? How can I get peace?' I start with myself and my problem, and as certainly as I do that when I am considering this doctrine of sanctification, I am sure, in some shape or form, to end by regarding God as merely an agency who is there to help me to solve my problem. And this is a totally unscriptural approach to the almighty ever blessed God.

There was a book, written in the 1930s by a distinguished American preacher, who, incidentally, was a Roman Catholic, with the startling title, *Religion without God*. The contents of the book were equally startling, because they were so terribly true. In many ways religion may be our greatest danger. We can worship religion, and we can be very religious without God. I mean by that, that we can be very punctilious in the observance of days and times and seasons. We can fast, we can deny ourselves things, and the whole time we are just centring upon ourselves and thinking about how we are going to improve ourselves and make ourselves better. We are trying to get certain lessons for ourselves, and the whole thing may be really self-centred. We may be highly religious, but there may be no place for God; or even if he does come in, he is simply there as someone who may be of help to us. We are at the centre of our religion; our religion really is a religion without God. And that is, I suppose, the last, and the ultimate, sin.

However, if we pay attention to these truths about which our Lord speaks we find that kind of position or attitude is a complete impossibility, because the first truth of sanctification, according to the Scriptures, is the truth of God himself. A very convenient way, I find, of realising that and of getting it fixed in my mind, is to look at it as follows. The condition, or the state, of sanctification (let me remind you once more that it is a condition and a state and not merely an experience) is, of course, the antithesis of the condition and the state of sin. Sanctification is that which separates us from sin unto God, whereas sin, ultimately, is to forget God. The essence of sin does not reside in the particular thing that I do, but rather in refusing to glorify God as he should be glorified. And all these sinful actions of ours are the manifestations of that central disease which is forgetfulness of God.

That is why sin is sometimes defined very rightly as self-centredness. It is selfishness. Sin really means that instead of living unto, and for God, and in the way that God desires of us, we are living for ourselves, in our own way, forgetful of him, and after the manner and the fashion of this world. So clearly, therefore, sanctification must of necessity start with this – my relationship to God. The first thing is not my getting rid of this particular sin that is in my life. No! The first thing must be God and my relationship to him. That is why the Bible always, everywhere, starts with God, and that is why we say once more that sanctification is really that condition or state in which a man lives his life continually under God and for God, and for his glory.

In other words, the main characteristic of people who are sanctified is that God is in the centre of their lives. That is the first thing we may say about them. Before we get them to say what they do or do not do with regard to a particular action, we must be clear about the central, primary, most vital thing, which is how the truth sanctifies us. It starts by holding us face to face with God and it tells us the truth about him. The Bible is primarily a revelation of God. It is not primarily interested in man, but in God. It is designed to bring man to a knowledge of God, and so it tells us about him.

And here again we must be careful to take the whole truth, because with our subjectivity we tend to be interested in God only from the standpoint of what we want, so that there is always a tendency to think of God only as a Saviour. But the Bible tells us much more about God than that. It gives us a revelation of the whole truth about God. We cannot take in the whole revelation, but the whole is good. So it tells us about God as Creator as well as God as Saviour. It tells us about his greatness, his majesty, his might and his dominion. It tells us something about the attributes of God. My friends, I am sure that as I bring these things before you, you will agree with me when I repeat once more, startling and surprising though it sounds at first, that the main difficulty with every one of us is that we forget God, and fail to realise who God is. It is because of this subjectivity of ours that we fail to realise, even when we are engaged in prayer, what we are doing and whom we are approaching. We are so concerned about our desires and our petitions that we fail to worship God, and to come to him in the way that the Scriptures everywhere tell us to approach him.

Consider the message of Hebrews 9 and 10. The great theme there is just this question of how to approach God. You go to the Old Testament and you see all that ritual and ceremonial – was it meaningless? Why were all these details given about the building of the Tabernacle and of the Temple? Why were the priests told to present certain offerings and sacrifices? Is this all meaningless? No! The answer is that it is all designed to teach man how to approach God, how to worship him. The shekinah glory was something real and absolute, and people could not rush into the Holiest of all whenever they liked. Only one man went in, the High Priest alone, and then only once a year, and then always with an offering of blood. The whole of the Old Testament, in a sense, is just this great teaching about how we are to approach God.

'Ah yes,' says someone, 'but wait a minute, that is the Old Testament. Do you not realise that Christ having come, every-thing is entirely different?' It is different in this way, that we are no longer dependent upon the Levitical ceremonial, and that in our Lord, we have the 'great High Priest'. But let us never forget that the New Testament, in the full light of the revela-tion of the Lord Jesus Christ, still goes on emphasising the importance of realising what we do when we approach God. The fact that I do not go into the 'Holiest of all' in the elaborate way in which the ancients went, but that I go in Christ, does not mean that I therefore need any less reverence! Let us approach God with reverence, and with godly fear, for 'our God is a consuming fire' (Heb 12:29).

The Scripture therefore promotes our sanctification, our holiness, by reminding us about all this; that the God whom we approach and whom we worship is the Creator of the uni-verse, the sustainer of everything. There is no end to his might and his majesty, to his dominion and his power. The Scripture emphasises God's holiness in a very special way. No one ever emphasised that more than the Lord Jesus Christ himself – you never hear him pray, 'dear Lord', or 'dear Father' but rather, 'holy Father'! That is the prayer of the one who was without sin at all, and who was absolutely perfect. When he approaches God, he addresses him as 'holy Father'! This is the truth that sanctifies, the truth that reminds us that God is in heaven and that we are on the earth; the truth that puts us into the right position and setting before God.

The greatest need of all of us is the need to be humble; our greatest lack is humility. It is our whole approach to God that is wrong, and the first great truth that we need to be taught is this truth that overrides everything else in the word of God. It is the truth about God's holiness, about God's eternal judgements and about his absolute righteousness. It is the truth that God is the Judge eternal. 'Ah but,' you say, 'I am a Christian and I am surely not concerned about judgement.' The Bible does not tell you that. The whole epistle to the Hebrews is a warning that we must meet God as Judge, and as Judge eternal. He is the one who shook the earth and who has now shaken the heavens. He is the judge of all men, and we must all appear before him.

That is a part of the truth of sanctification; it is not something that need only be preached in an evangelistic meeting. It is of the very essence of sanctification, and is its first principle. Our God is a consuming fire! John puts it this way, in teaching sanctification in his epistle. The first thing he lays down concerning sanctification is this: 'God is light, and in him is no darkness at all' (1 Jn 1:5); so I suggest to you that we have no right to go on to consider any other aspects whatsoever of the truth of sanctification until we have realised that truth. And then John, having started with this emphasis concerning the truth about God, especially stresses in following verses that salvation is God's plan.

Here again let me put this negatively. Are we not sometimes prone to think that salvation really is something that arises

from man; that God is just waiting passively for us to go to
him, and that when we do go and ask him for certain things, he
will be graciously pleased to give them to us? Our tendency is
to think of salvation only from our side. But the Bible puts it
solely on the other side. Salvation and heaven are the plan of
God. They are the scheme of God. They come from God and
originate with him.

The Bible tells us that God's great purpose in salvation is to
separate unto himself a 'peculiar people, zealous of good
works' (Tit 2:14). Everything that has been done in this great
design of salvation – every aspect, every movement, every vision of it – is all designed for that end. I have always found that
nothing has helped me with this whole question of sanctification so much as the realisation that I am simply someone who,
as a Christian, has been taken into this scheme and plan of God.
For instead of thinking primarily of myself and of my problems and of my needs and of my desires, I have awakened to
the glorious, stupendous, thrilling fact that the great God who
has planned this scheme of salvation has looked upon me, and
has brought me into that scheme. So I do not start thinking of
myself as myself; I see myself in God's plan and in God's purpose.

You will notice that I am repeating this because it seems to
me that not to realise this is the root cause of most troubles.
Kierkegaard, the great Danish theologian, who lived in the last
century, coined a phrase which has been very popular in our
own days. He said that 'religion is subjectivity'. He lived in a
country where you had orthodox Lutheranism which had been
dead and petrified for a long time. The teaching was perfectly
orthodox, they never said anything that was wrong, but it was
lifeless. Kierkegaard saw that such orthodoxy was of no value.
He said that merely to hold a number of correct intellectual
notions and subscribe to a number of correct propositions was
not religion. 'That is not what I find in the Bible,' he wrote.
'That is not what I find in the lives of the saints. They had
something vital, something living, something had happened to
them.' So he said that 'religion is subjectivity'.

He was, of course, over-emphasising. He wanted to shock the people out of their dead orthodoxy. He was right in this, but in the end he went too far. It is always the danger when we try to correct an error. The danger, if we are not careful, is always that we start by speaking out in a striking manner that will shock people out of one error and end by going into another error, which is the exact opposite of the one we are correcting. If Kierkegaard had said that in religion there must always be a subjective element, he would have been right, but when he says that 'religion is subjectivity' he is wrong.

So it would be equally wrong for me to maintain that 'religion is objectivity', and I am not saying that. But what I am saying is that as you tend to need particular emphases at different times and in different epochs, I have no hesitation at all in saying that the emphasis that is needed at the present time is objective, because we are all so subjective in our approach, and we forget God. The truth is that we must start with the objective fact and truth of God, and then think of it as ours in relation to that – our object and our objective. It must be both. It is neither one nor the other; it is both one and the other. It is the objective eternal truth outside myself, God's plan of salvation; and also it is the fact that I myself am brought into that, so that I am aware of God dealing with me, and of things happening to me.

But my emphasis here is that we must start with God and the fact of God, and not simply with our own subjective moods, our own states and feelings and our own personal needs and problems. That then is the truth in general. But there are certain particular emphases that I want also to mention. What is holiness? Well, I do not know a better definition than this: 'Thou shalt love the Lord thy God with all thy heart, and with all thy soul, and with all thy mind, and with all thy strength' (Mk 12:30). *That* is holiness.

For holiness is not simply to have certain problems solved in your life, because you may get certain sins taken from your life and still be far removed from holiness. Essential holiness is a condition in which a man loves God with his heart and his soul and his mind and his strength, and the greater the degree or the proportion of each part of the personality that is engaged in this love, the greater the sanctification. Thus, to be sanctified does not just mean that you are not committing certain sins while you are enjoying that particular experience. No, that is a negative view; that is a corollary.

The essence of sanctification is that I love the God in whom I believe, and who has been revealed to me, with the whole of my being. Indeed I do not hesitate to assert that if I think of sanctification in any lesser terms that that, I am being unscriptural. This is scriptural holiness. This is the holiness, the sanctification, that is produced and promoted by the truth of God, because it is the truth concerning God. Then it follows from that – I think directly – that a man who does thus love God with all his heart and soul and mind and strength does so because he is called upon to do so and is commanded to do so. To such a man the main thing in life is to glorify God and to show forth his praises.

This is the argument of the apostle Peter when he reminds the people to whom he is writing that at one time before they became Christians they were not a people. 'Which in time past,' he says, in 1 Peter 1:10, 'were not a people but are now the people of God.' You who are called out of darkness into light are a 'peculiar people'. Why? What is the object of it all? 'That ye should shew forth the praises of him who hath called you out of darkness into his marvellous light' (1 Pet 2:9). 'Praises' there means 'excellencies' or 'virtues'; it means the glorious, marvellous attributes of God. And so, sanctification is that condition in which we praise God just by being what we are. Of course, it includes not doing certain things, but it is not only that. It is much more. By being what we are in all the totality of our personalities and in the whole of our lives, we reveal and manifest the virtues and the excellencies of God. God, of course, calls us to do that. The whole of the biblical teaching about our sonship of God in Christ, is the same argument. 'Be ye holy,' says God, 'for I am holy.' My reason for being holy must not be that I stop committing that sin so that I shall not suffer remorse and have the need of repentance, and that I shall not be miserable and unhappy. Not at all! I am to be holy because God is holy.

Is that not the teaching right through the Bible, in the Old as well as in the New Testament? Why did God give the children of Israel the Ten Commandments? Why did he tell them in detail what to do and what not to do? The reason he always gave was: You are my people; you are unlike all the other nations. I have adopted you; I have taken you; I have created you. You are my people. I want you to live as my people. I want everybody to know that you are my people. Let your life be such that everybody will know that you are God's people. 'Be ye holy for I am holy.' It is exactly the same in the New Testament. 'Let your light so shine before men [or, among men] that they may see your good works and glorify your Father which is in heaven' (Mt 5:16). 'That is the way you must live,' says our Lord in effect in the Sermon on the Mount, 'that is how I am living. I live in such a way that people see me glorifying my Father.' And when he performed his miracles, people praised and glorified God.

And you and I must live like that. That is sanctification, and it is, of course, impossible unless we understand the truth about God. We must realise that our whole life is meant to be lived to the glory of God. The whole purpose of salvation is to make us such that we shall glorify him, and therefore the test of sanctification is not the giving up of my sins, nor my happiness, nor whether I have sacrificed so much in my life; rather, it is whether I am indeed concerned to live only and entirely to the glory of God.

One further point that we must make is that the essence of the Christian life is that we have fellowship and communion with God. Our Lord has already said in John 17, 'This is life eternal, that they might know thee the only true God, and Jesus Christ whom thou hast sent.' As Christians, then, our first and great claim is that we 'know' God, that we 'know' the Lord Jesus Christ. The privilege that we enjoy as Christian people is hat we are in fellowship with God, we are in union with him. Therefore, say the Scriptures, realise who he is and what he s. The apostle John works out the argument for us in his first pistle. The Christian life, he says, is essentially one of walking vith God in this life. Therefore, 'If we say that we have fellowhip with him, and walk in darkness, we lie, and do not the ruth' (1 Jn 1:6). He goes further in the second chapter and says, He that saith, I know him, and keepeth not his commandnents, is a liar, and the truth is not in him' (2:14).

John's basic definition of sanctification is clear. He teaches that it is the knowledge of God which leads to a life that corresponds with that knowledge. In other words, we are interested in the commandments. How often, I wonder, have you heard the Ten Commandments preached in sanctification and holiness meetings? But we must keep them; it is a part of the preaching, and of the truth, it is the word that sanctifies. It is the truth about God, because to be sanctified is to be walking in his fellowship, realising what we are doing, and living to his glory. So it is still the truth about God which is applied in our lives, and the result of all this is that we begin to understand what the apostle Paul means when he says, 'Work out your own salvation with fear and trembling' (Phil 2:12).

'Oh,' you say, 'but I thought the truth about sanctification was that it is that which delivers me from fear and trembling, that which makes me happy, and which takes the struggle out of my life.' But we must 'work out', and 'with fear and trembling' because sanctification means essentially that we are in this relationship with God, and that we realise what it means. It is not a craven fear – it is the reverence and the godly fear spoken about by the author of the epistle to the Hebrews (12:28–29). It is the fear of wounding or of offending or of hurting such holiness and such love. It is the fear of marring God's purpose and plan, his scheme and his perfect work that is going on in me, for he works in me both to will and to do.

Let me summarise it all by putting it like this. I notice that the Bible itself always describes sanctification in terms of 'godliness' and 'holiness' and 'righteousness'. I do not see that the characteristic biblical description of the sanctified life is 'victorious living' or 'the life of victory' or 'overcoming'. We are familiar with these terms, are we not? They have come in, in recent years. But the Bible describes sanctification in terms of godliness, god-likeness; that is its biblical term – holiness which is a description of God himself.

We tend to describe sanctification as the 'victorious life' because we think of it in terms of getting rid of particular sins. 'How am I to get victory over this sin? How am I to get victory in my life?' Again, you see, I am starting with myself – I want victory. But the Bible describes it in terms of my relationship to God. How often do you hear the term 'holiness' used today? How often do you hear men described as 'god-fearing' men? Those were the biblical terms; until comparatively recently those were the great evangelical terms. But the whole outlook has changed. We have become subjective, and I would suggest to you that, to that extent, we have become unscriptural.

Of course, if we are godly we shall have our victories; but if you describe sanctification only in terms of 'victories' you have got the negative view. If you describe it in terms of 'holiness' and 'godliness' and 'god-likeness' and 'righteousness', then your view will always be positive. And though you may not be guilty of certain sins, you will still see yourself as a sinner; you will still be dissatisfied, but you will press on; you will still strive; you will still reckon yourself dead to sin; you will still go on reaching after holiness, hungering and thirsting after righteousness. Whereas if you only look at it in terms of victory, the great danger is to be self-satisfied and content, to be smug, and to lead a superficial, incomplete and inadequate Christian life.

The first message, the first aspect of truth, the truth which sanctifies, is God – the holy, righteous, eternal, ever-blessed God, who, in Jesus Christ, has become my Father, and with whom I can walk while I am left in this life, and with whom I shall spend my eternity. Let us ever approach him with reverence and godly fear. Let us remember that godlikeness is the end we strive for.

# 8

## The Truth about Sin

*Sanctify them through thy truth: thy word is truth (v. 17).*

Thus far we have seen that the specific plan and purpose of everything that God has been graciously pleased to do in and through his only begotten Son, is to bring us to a knowledge of himself. Our Lord has stated that very plainly in this great chapter that we are considering together: 'This is life eternal, that they might know thee the only true God, and Jesus Christ, whom thou hast sent.' And whatever we may have experienced, whatever may have happened to us, if we have not this knowledge of God, then it is doubtful whether we are in a position of salvation at all; and there is certainly no value to any moral or ethical qualities that may belong to us unless they derive centrally from this knowledge. So we have seen that we must start with the doctrine of God.

And now we come to the second great section of the truth, which is, of course, the one that follows by a kind of inevitability and logical necessity from the doctrine of God, namely, the doctrine of sin. We must now consider what the word has to tell us about sin and about ourselves in a state and a condition of sin. If, as I say, salvation ultimately means to know God, then the great problem for us is to know what it is that separates us from God. The biblical answer to that is not that it is a lack of natural capacity, nor is it a philosophical inability. No, the one thing that comes between any one of us

95

and God is sin, and that is the great doctrine which you find running right through the Bible.

Here again is an aspect of the truth which for some reason we tend to neglect. I feel that we can say about this doctrine of sin what I once heard a man say about the observance of the Lord's Day. He said he had come to the conclusion that the Lord's Day, like the Lord himself, was in danger of dying between two thieves, the two thieves being Saturday night and Monday morning! He said that increasingly Saturday night was extended and extended, and blended into Sunday, and then people started their Monday morning quite early on Sunday evening. Sunday becomes just a few hours during the morning, and then we think, 'Well, that is enough now, we have been to church once.' Thus our Lord's Day has been lost between two thieves.

I feel that it is equally true to say something like that about this biblical doctrine of sin, and it seems to me to be happening in this way. When we are dealing with the unconverted, we tend to say: 'Ah, you need not worry about sin now, that will come later. All you need to do is to come to Christ, to give yourself to Christ. Do not worry your head about sin – of course you cannot understand that now. Do not worry either whether or not you have got a sense of sin or deep conviction, or whether you know these things. All you need to do is to come to Christ, to give yourself to Christ, and then you will be happy.'

Then when we are dealing with those who have so come, our tendency, again, is to say to them, 'Of course, you must not look at yourself, you must look to Christ. You must not be for ever analysing yourself. That is wrong, that is what you did before you were converted. You were thinking in terms of yourself and of what you had got to do. The only thing you must do is to keep looking to Christ and away from yourself.' We imagine, therefore, that all that is needed by Christians is a certain amount of comfort and encouragement, of preaching about the love of God and about his general providence and perhaps a certain amount of moral and ethical exhortation. And so, you see, the doctrine of sin is, as it were, crowded out. We fail to emphasise it both before and after conversion, and the result is that we hear very little about it.

Now whether you agree with my explanation or not, I think we must all agree with the fact that the doctrine of sin has been sadly neglected. We know that instinctively. We none of us like it, and thus it comes to pass that this doctrine is so little emphasised. And yet when you come to the Bible you find it everywhere, and for this reason, it should of necessity be central. Why should anybody come to Christ? What do people do when they come to him? What do they mean when they say they believe on him? How can that possibly happen apart from some understanding of sin? You cannot give yourself, or your heart to Christ, you cannot surrender, you cannot use the term, 'Take him as your Saviour', unless you know what he is to save you from.

So it is surely utterly unscriptural to indulge in any sort of evangelism which neglects the doctrine of sin. There is no real meaning or content to the term 'Saviour' or 'salvation' apart from the doctrine of sin, which has this tremendous emphasis throughout the Bible. Our fathers – perhaps I should say our grandfathers, and those who preceded them, they of the older evangelicalism – always laid great emphasis on what they called our 'law work'. They emphasised the importance of a thorough-going preliminary law work before you came to the gospel and its redemption, and they were distrustful of those who claimed salvation except in those terms. And as you read their lives you will find they have a great deal to say about 'the plague of their own hearts'. If you read of saintly men like Robert Murray McCheyne, and men of that generation, and those who preceded them, the men of the eighteenth century, you will find that that was their terminology. But it is a language which has somehow or other dropped out, and I think it has done so in the way I have indicated.

But after all, whatever they may have said and thought, the fact which confronts us is that this is something which is found in the Bible everywhere, in the Old Testament and the New, one cannot ignore it, and it is for that reason that we must consider it. I suggest that it is absolutely vital to a true understanding of sanctification that we should know something about the biblical doctrine of sin. It is only as we realise the truth about ourselves and our condition, it is only as we come to realise our ultimate need, that we apply to Christ, who alone can supply it. In other words, there is nothing in our experience that so drives us to Christ as the realisation of our need and our helplessness.

> Foul, I to the fountain fly;
> Wash me, Saviour, or I die.

It is because I am foul that I fly to the fountain, and if I do not realise my need of being washed I will not go there.

> Naked, come to Thee for dress;
> Helpless, look to Thee for grace.
>
> *Augustus Toplady*

These things of necessity go together. 'They that be whole need not a physician, but they that are sick' (Mt 9:12). You do not go to your doctor if you feel perfectly well. You never make an application for any kind of healing or redemption or salvation unless you are conscious of your need. And that, of course, is the whole trouble with the world today – it does not realise this need; that is why it does not believe in the Lord Jesus Christ.

But the same thing is true in principle of the Christian. It is those who realise their condition and their need most deeply who are the ones who apply most constantly to the Lord himself. This is the universal testimony of the saints. It does not matter where they lived, or to what century they belonged. You read the life of any saint of God, anyone who so stood out in saintliness that somebody felt it right and good and fitting that a biography should be written of him or her, and you will find that invariably this has been a characteristic of such a person. If you read their lives and their diaries, you will find that they bemoaned the fact that they were aware of indwelling sin, this 'plague of their own heart' as they called it, this thing in them that so often vitiated their testimony and hampered what they really desired to do and to be for the Lord. It is invariably those who have testified to the most high and glorious experiences, who at the same time testify to this other thing. Indeed the life of the Christian seems to be some sort of an ellipse which runs between these two focal points. At one and the same time you always find in the saint a hearty detestation of, and misery about, self, and yet a rejoicing and a joy in the Lord; and the one of necessity determines the other.

But let us be a little more particular. This is the truth which the word of God teaches us. It teaches us about God, then about sin, and that is the way in which it sanctifies us. There are several ways in which the word of God presents this particular aspect of the truth. I am not going to deal with it exhaustively, but let me give you some of the more obvious and general divisions.

The first way in which the Scriptures do this is, of course, through the teaching of the law – the law of God. There is much about the law of God in the Bible. It was originally given to man in the Garden of Eden, and the Scriptures tell us that there is a law written in the heart of every person born into this world. In Romans 2 Paul teaches that even the heathen, who have never heard the Scripture about the law of God, have it written in their hearts. It is also in the Bible, in a very special way, in terms of the Law which was given through Moses to the Children of Israel. You find the account given in the book of Exodus, there are constant references to it in the Psalms, and the subject also runs right through the Proverbs. These passages are in a sense doing nothing but applying this Law that was given, reminding the nation of it. It is everywhere in the Old Testament, and, indeed, it is true to say that we just cannot understand the Old Testament and its religion unless we are clear about the place and the function of the law of God in it.

Then you come to the New Testament and there again you will find constant arguments concerning the law. But what is their purpose, if we do not really understand what the law is? Now the law is given primarily in order to bring out these two points: the holiness of God and the sinfulness of man in the light of that holiness. It is interesting to observe in this connection the way in which the Jews completely misunderstood that. Their real trouble, as Paul is never tired of arguing, was that they had entirely misinterpreted the meaning of the law. They thought its purpose was to save them; that God had given them the law and said to them in effect, 'Now you keep that, and you will be saved. You save yourselves by keeping the law.' They had conveniently misinterpreted it; then they carried out that misinterpretation and said that they had kept the law and were righteous before God. That was the very essence of their error.

The purpose and the function of the law was really, as Paul argues in Romans 7, to show the exceeding sinfulness of sin, 'Was then that which is good made death unto me? God forbid. But sin, that it might appear sin, working death in me by that which is good; that sin by the commandment might become exceeding sinful' (v. 13). The law was not given in order to save man or that man might save himself by it. It was given for one purpose only, namely, that sin might be defined, that it might, as it were, have attention focused upon it. Mankind did not realise its sinfulness, so God gave the law, not that they might save themselves by keeping it, but that their very sinfulness could be brought out. The law is 'our school-master to bring us unto Christ' (Gal 3:24), that is its only function, to show us our helplessness, and our need of grace and of a free salvation. 'Therefore by the deeds of the law there shall no flesh be justified in his sight: for by the law is the knowledge of sin' (Rom 3:20).

Those, then, are some of the scriptural statements, and all this great teaching about the law is simply to bring out in us a sense of sin. Therefore it follows of necessity that if we have never really studied this biblical doctrine, if we have never applied it to ourselves, if we are not doing so constantly, then we are not as aware of our own sinfulness as we should be. That is what the Fathers meant by a 'thorough-going law work'. It is only as I truly face the law of God that I begin to see what I am.

We see this, too, in the Sermon on the Mount. In its essence this Sermon is an explanation and an exposition of God's law.

It is our Lord showing us the real spiritual content of the law, demonstrating the law's spiritual nature, denouncing the false interpretation of the Pharisees, and really bringing us to see what it is telling us. And he does so, surely, with the object of bringing us to realise our sinfulness. The aim of the Sermon on the Mount is to disabuse us of all ideas about human self-righteousness. It is an exposure of the Pharisees and Scribes and of all who tended to follow them. In a sense, its whole purpose is to bring us into a condition in which we shall be 'poor in spirit', in which we shall 'mourn', in which we shall 'hunger and thirst after righteousness'. That is its obvious appeal. It is to bring us into the position and the state of those who are described by the Beatitudes.

Again, we find the same teaching in the epistles. That is the meaning of these discussions and arguments about the law, and of terms such as the 'old man', and the 'new man', and 'flesh' and the 'law of sin and death' and so on. You find this constantly in the epistles, particularly, perhaps, you find it in their exhortations. These are made in order that the people should examine themselves and 'prove' themselves, to make certain that they are in the faith; to 'test the spirits'; to avoid the false and to hold fast to that which is true. All that is part of the teaching concerning sin.

That, therefore, in general, is the way in which you find this doctrine about sin presented in the Scriptures. And that leads me to ask my second question. What in particular is the teaching about sin? Now obviously I am dealing with it here solely from the standpoint of the Christian. I should be emphasising certain other things if I were presenting it to the unbeliever, but I am particularly concerned now about the biblical teaching concerning sin with regard to God's people. And here there are certain principles which stand out very clearly.

The first is the vital and essential difference between sin and sins. The main trouble with a false doctrine of sin is that it tends to make us think of sin only in terms of actions. There have been many schools of false teaching about holiness, which have been wrong entirely because they have defined sin in that way, and, therefore, have taught that as long as we are not guilty of voluntary, wilful sin, we are perfect, we are entire and fully sanctified.

But the Bible draws a very sharp distinction between particular actions and a sinful state and condition, and its emphasis is not so much upon what we do, as upon what we are, upon the condition we are in, which leads us to do these things. That is a broad principle which it lays down everywhere.

So, to put it the other way round, the biblical emphasis is on being rather than doing. It is a positive state. True Christians are not so much people who do certain things, as people who *are* something, and because of what they are, then they do those things. Another way the Bible puts this important principle is in its teachings that sin, primarily, is a wrong attitude towards God, and a wrong relationship with him. Again you see that it defines sin not merely in terms of the moral, ethical character of the action. On the contrary, it goes further back and shows that in its essence sin is a wrong relationship with God and a wrong attitude towards him. Therefore sin, defined comprehensively, is anything or everything that prevents our living only to God, for him, and for his glory.

Those who say that sin ultimately means self are, of course, perfectly right. They are right as far as they go, but they do not go far enough. Sin is self, self-centredness and selfishness. But the real trouble about selfishness is not so much that I am self-centred, as that I am not God-centred. You see, you can have philosophical, and moral and ethical teachings which will denounce selfishness. All the idealistic systems, all the programmes for Utopia, are always very careful to denounce self-centredness. Obviously you cannot have a well-ordered society if everybody is out for himself or herself. There must be give and take. You agree that you must consider the other person, and that you must put in certain limits on your freedom in order that the other person may enjoy freedom. So you can denounce self as such, and still be far removed from the biblical doctrine of sin. Self in all its forms is sinful, says the Bible, because it puts self where God ought to be.

Now if you start with that definition of sin you see how comprehensive it becomes! Take that Pharisee, for instance, who thanked God that he was not like other people. Up to a point he was quite honest and truthful in what he said. He was not guilty of certain things, and he did other things. Yes. But he stopped at that. If he had realised that the essence of sin is to fail to be in the right relationship to God, or to have the right attitude towards God, he would have realised his sinfulness. There are many Christian people who are very careful not to commit certain external sins, but they are not quite so careful about pride and self-satisfaction, and about smugness and glibness; they are not so careful about rivalry and jealousy in their own Christian organisations. No, they have forgotten all that. Self is in the ascendant, at times even in their work, instead of God. But because they think of sin only in terms of actions, and have forgotten that it is primarily relationship to God, they are not aware of their sinfulness. However, that is the very essence of sin – failing to live entirely and wholly to God's glory. And it matters not how good we may be, nor how much better we may be than other people. If we are not loving the Lord our God with all our heart, and all our soul, and all our mind, and all our strength, then we are sinners. 'All have sinned, and come short of the glory of God' (Rom 3:23). That is the biblical teaching.

Then the other great principle is that sin is something which is deep down in our natures; it is not something on the surface. It is not a lack of culture, or of knowledge, or of instruction. Nor is it like a little speck on the surface of an otherwise perfect apple. No, it is at the centre, at the very core. It is not merely something in the stream, but at the fountain out of which the stream comes. It is something which is central to a man's being.

This, again, is emphasised everywhere in the Scripture. Paul refers to it as a principle. It is the whole meaning of the term 'the flesh', which does not mean the physical body, but that principle in a man's life that tends to control him. Indeed the Bible says that sin is so deep in man that nothing can possibly rid him of it, or deliver him from it, except a rebirth. Teaching is not enough, neither are exhortation, nor example. Even the example of Christ is not enough; in a sense it damns more than anything else. There is only one hope, says the Scripture: you must be 'born again'. You must be made and created anew. Sin is so deep down in man himself that he needs a new nature. Sin indeed is as deep a problem as this – that nothing but the Incarnation and all that our Lord did, can possibly deal with it. And so we must realise that though we are Christians and have received a new nature, the problem is still there because of the remnants of old nature. We have not finished with it.

There, I suggest, are the three main controlling principles. But we must still divide that up just a little further. If that is the truth about sin, we must ask the question, How, then, does it show itself? So we turn to the teaching of the Bible. First and foremost, sin is what is always described as 'missing the mark', not being at the place where you ought to be. You are shooting and you just miss the mark; or you are travelling and you do not arrive at the exact destination. That is the very essence of the biblical understanding of sin. It is an absence of righteousness and of holiness. Every sinner is not what he ought to be, and not what he was when he came out of the hands of God. We are not reflecting the glory of God as we were meant to do. We are not as we were when man was made in God's image. The image has been marred. Something has gone.

You see the importance of regarding sin in that way. The man who realises that that is a primary part of the definition of sin, is a man who realises that he is still a sinner. But if you are simply looking at drunkards and prostitutes, or at particular actions, of course you think that you are all right. You are not conscious of sin, so you are not humble and you do not 'mourn'. You are self-satisfied and contented; you are looking down at other people. But once you realise that we are meant to be holy and righteous, and that we are not that, then you realise at once that you are a sinner.

But sin is not only this negative condition of not being righteous and holy, it is also a positive transgression of the law. Consider John's argument about that in 1 John 3, '... for sin is the transgression of the law' (v. 4). Sin is disobedience to God's commandments, and the Bible emphasises this quite as much as the negative. Our trouble is not only that we are not what we ought to be, but that we deliberately do things that we should not do. It is a breaking of the law, a transgression, a cutting across what God has indicated as being his holy will.

Yes, but it is something even worse than that. It is what is described as 'concupiscence'. We find this word in Romans 7 and it is something that we must always preach. 'But sin, taking occasion by the commandment, wrought in me all manner of concupiscence. For without the law sin was dead' (v.8). This is the biblical way of describing desire – evil desire. The trouble is not simply that we break the law and do things that are wrong, the trouble is also that we ever want to do so; that it ever gives us pleasure to do these things; that there ever is an inclination in us to do them; that there is something in us which makes such disobedience appeal to us – that is an element in concupiscence.

But it is even worse than that. Concupiscence is as terrible and as foul a thing as this, that even the law of God inflames us. Look at Paul's argument in Romans 7. He says,

> For when we were in the flesh, the motions of sins, which were by the law, did work in our members to bring forth fruit unto death. But now we are delivered from the law, that being dead wherein we were held; that we should serve in newness of spirit, and not in the oldness of the letter. What shall we say then? Is the law sin? God forbid. Nay, I had not known sin, but by the law: for I had not known lust, except the law had said, Thou shalt not covet. But sin, taking occasion by the commandment, wrought in me all manner of concupiscence. For without the law sin was dead. For I was alive without the law once: but when the commandment came, sin revived, and I died. And the commandment, which was ordained to life, I found to be unto death. For sin, taking occasion by the commandment, deceived me, and by it slew me. Wherefore the law is holy, and the commandment holy, and just, and good. Was then that which is good made death unto me? God forbid. But sin, that it might appear sin, working death in me by that which is good; that sin by the commandment might become exceeding sinful' (vv. 5–13).

Paul's argument is as follows. There is this terrible thing called concupiscence in man, and it works in this way. You tell a man, a child, indeed anybody, not to do a thing. Now, it is a good thing to tell people not to do what is wrong, and to do what is good. Yes, says Paul, but this is what I have found, and we have all found the same thing, that the very commandment which tells me not to do that evil thing, by drawing my attention to it, inflames my desire to do it. So that the very law leads me to sin. It is not because the law is not right and good and just and holy. God forbid, he says, that anybody should say that. The problem is this evil thing in me called concupiscence, which will even turn good into evil. To the pure all things are pure. To those who are not pure there is nothing good.

That is why as a Christian I have never believed in morality teaching. Nor have I ever agreed with those who argue, 'Tell people of the evil effects of that sin, and it will keep them from it,' because it will not. It will inflame their desire for that very thing that you are telling them not to do. And that is why people quite often delude and defile themselves by reading books about such things. They say that what they want to do is to see the evil of the thing. What is actually happening is that they are enjoying it. They are sinning in their minds and in their imaginations. That is what is meant by concupiscence; this passion, this flame, this fire, that can even misuse the law of God, and turn it into a kind of bellows that makes the flame worse. Tell a man not to and it may drive him to do it – indeed, you are introducing him to it. So it is a dangerous thing for fallen man to think like that and to imagine that moral instruction about sex and such things is going to control the moral problem. It is having exactly the opposite effect; and to believe in that kind of teaching is to misunderstand the essential biblical teaching about sin. No, our fathers were right. They did not tell their children about sex and morality, and there was less immorality than there is now. It is a dangerous thing to talk about these things; it is like pouring petrol on the fire. Concupiscence – that is the great argument of the seventh chapter of the epistle to the Romans.

Finally, I must put it in these words. Sin shows itself, says Paul, as a kind of law in my life and in my members. You will notice he talks about the 'law in his members' – 'For I delight in the law of God after the inward man: but I see another law in my members, warring against the law of my mind, and bringing me into captivity to the law of sin which is in my members' (Rom 7:22–23). That is sin, with its terrible power. It is a great principle. It is a law, says Paul, and it works in this way: even though we may know that the law of God is right and good and just and holy, and though we believe in it and even want to keep it, we find that we are doing something else. Why? Because there is another law in our members, this thing called the flesh.

Paul therefore comes to the conclusion that '…in me (that is, in my flesh) dwelleth no good thing' (Rom 7:18). As I have said, Paul does not mean the physical body, but this principle of sin, this law of sin, this law in the members. They are all synonymous terms. It is this thing that governs man, so that though I want to do the right thing, and subscribe to it and love it, I nevertheless find myself doing the other thing. That, as I see it, is the biblical teaching in its essence with regard to sin – and we know it is true.

But how often do we think about this? How often do we meditate upon it? How often do we search ourselves and examine ourselves to see how guilty we are? Are we dismissing these things lightly, pushing them away, not really facing them? The Scripture exhorts us to face them: that is why it puts the law before us everywhere. We need to be kept down. We need to be humbled. We need to be convicted of sin.

And it is only as we are, that we shall realise the need of sanctification. It is only as we are, that we shall apply to Christ and seek his face and seek God. It is only as we are, that we shall thank God that the whole of salvation, from beginning to end, is God's work and not ours. It will deliver us out of this superficial dealing with the problem in terms of actions. It will enable us to see our true condition as sold under sin, and covered by the law of sin and death. Then we will know that we are doomed and condemned and hopeless, and needing that mighty operation of the Spirit of God which, blessed be his name, gives us new life and new birth, and then proceeds by the application of this blessed word in us and upon us, to perfect us until eventually, because it is his work and his power, we shall stand before him faultless and blameless, and with exceeding joy.

God grant that we may understand the biblical teaching – the word of God's teaching about sin – that it may drive us to Christ.

# 9

## New Creatures

*Sanctify them through thy truth: thy word is truth (v. 17).*

We continue now in our consideration of God's way of sanctifying his people, and of the fact that the great emphasis here is that God sanctifies us not so much directly as indirectly, through and by means of the truth. He brings us into the realm of the truth in order that the truth may work upon us, and produce the desired effects and results in us. And therefore we see that the whole of the biblical message – and in a very special way the message of the New Testament – is designed to bring about this final purpose of our sanctification. For that reason we have been at pains to emphasise the unity of the truth and every part of the truth which leads to sanctification. The truth about sanctification is not some special department or one aspect of the teaching of the Bible. Every revelation of God, and everything that brings us to a realisation of our position in God's sight, leads to and produces our sanctification. So that it has been necessary for us to look at the truth as a whole, and we are now in the process of reminding ourselves that this great comprehensive truth has different aspects, or different emphases. And in accordance with the biblical message, we are looking at these different aspects of the truth which lead to our sanctification.

We started with the great truth about God himself. There is nothing more calculated to make a man holy and to sanctify him truly as the realisation that he is in the presence of God. There is no better definition of a true Christian than that he is a godly man, one who walks in the fear of the Lord. That is invariably the biblical description of God's people; clearly, it is the point at which we must start, because it is the centre and the soul of all truth. But then that, in turn, leads us, of course, to consider what the Bible has to tell us about sin. Why do we not all know God? Why are we not walking with him, and enjoying fellowship with him? The answer is sin. And the more we realise the exceeding sinfulness of sin, the more we shall hate it, abominate it, and turn our backs on it, and give ourselves unreservedly to God and to the life which he would have us live.

Then that obviously leads to the next emphasis. Having shown us our utter sinfulness and our complete helplessness, lest we give way to final despair, the Bible presents us with the wonderful truth about what the love of God has done in Christ for us and for our salvation. The great argument of Christ, finally, is that it is our sin which made that necessary, and that Christ died, not only that we might be forgiven, but that we might be delivered from sin.

> Love so amazing, so divine,
> Demands my soul, my life, my all.
>
> *Isaac Watts*

'Know ye not … ye are not your own? For ye are bought with a price' (1 Cor 6:19–20). '… he died for all, that they which live should not henceforth live unto themselves but unto him which died for them, and rose again' (2 Cor 5:15). If our understanding of the death of Christ upon the cross does not make us hate sin and forsake it, and hate the world and forsake the world, and give ourselves unreservedly to Christ, we are in the most dangerous condition possible. To imagine that Christ died on the cross simply to allow us to continue living a sinful and worldly life in safety, comes, it seems to me, very near a terrible form of blasphemy. There is no more dangerous condition for a soul to be in, than to think: 'Well, because I have believed in Christ and because I think that Christ died for me, it does not matter very much now what I do.' The whole of this message is an utter denial of that, and a solemn warning to us not to make merchandise of the cross of Christ, or to trample under our feet the blood of our redemption. So you see that every aspect of the truth drives us to holiness, and all the teaching urges us to sanctification.[1]

But now we come to another aspect of the truth, one which, again, is vital for our understanding of this subject. It warns us that we must be clear about our actual position as Christians as the result of the work of the Lord Jesus Christ on our behalf. Here again we have one of the major themes of the Bible and one of its major emphases with regard to this particular question of sanctification: the Christian's standing as the result of the work of the Lord Jesus Christ. It is a great theme which is expounded in many places in the New Testament, though I suppose the classic passage is Romans 6. However, it is not only in the sixth chapter of Romans; everything that leads up to this chapter is part of the argument, and it goes on in to the seventh. But in the sixth chapter this theme is presented to us in a particularly con-centrated form.

You will notice that the apostle takes up at once the whole question of the relationship between the meaning of the death of Christ upon the cross and our conduct. He imagines the people in Rome misunderstanding this teaching, as others had so often been liable to do. He imagines that they may say to themselves: 'Well, shall we continue in sin that grace may abound? Is this a teaching which says that now that we have believed in Christ we are no longer under the law but under grace, and that, therefore, it does not much matter what we do, indeed, that the more we sin the greater will be the grace? Is that the position?'

---

[1] Unfortunately, at this point one sermon is missing from the John 17 manuscripts. However, Dr Lloyd-Jones often gave a detailed resumé of the sermon of the week before, and we have left this in full, in order to show, however briefly, what the subject was of the missing manu-script, and how it connects with the sermons before and after. (Ed.)

Paul's answer is given with horror – 'God forbid!' God forbid that anybody should argue like that. 'How shall we, that are dead to sin, live any longer therein?' (6:2). The thing is unthinkable. It is a complete misunderstanding of the truth! So he works it out, and the important thing to grasp here is that all along he relates his doctrine to the practice of the Christian. You cannot separate these two things. For the extent to which there is a separation between what we believe, and what we are, and what we do, is the extent to which we have really not understood the doctrine; because there are certain things that are absolutely indivisible. That is why the New Testament is so full of tests which Christians must apply to themselves. There is the danger of our deluding ourselves and falsely imagining that we are Christians. The whole first epistle of John just deals with that one thing – the tests of the Christian life – the way in which we must examine ourselves. It is no use, said the Lord Jesus Christ, pleading, 'Lord, Lord' if you do not do and keep my commandments. 'Many will say to me in that day, Lord, Lord, have we not prophesied in thy name …?' (Mt 7:22). Have we not done this and that? And he will answer, 'I never knew you: depart from me …' (v. 23). They thought they believed in him. They said, 'Lord, Lord,' but he never knew them. So we must examine ourselves very carefully, and we do so by always keeping a firm grasp, at one and the same time, upon our doctrine and our practice and our conduct. Life and belief are indivisible; they must go together.

Now that is how the apostle Paul conducts this great argument in Romans 6, and I want to examine it with you in a very special manner here. The great principle, it seems to me, with which we must start is that an assurance of our salvation, of our standing before God, and of the forgiveness of our sins, is an absolute necessity in this matter of sanctification. Let me put it to you like this. I would not hesitate to say that a lack of assurance is perhaps one of the greatest hindrances of all in the Christian life, because while you have not got assurance you are troubled and worried, and that tends to lead to depression. It tends to turn us in upon ourselves, and to promote morbidity and introspection; and in that condition we obviously become a ready prey for the devil, who is ever at hand to discourage us and to suggest to us that we are not Christians at all.

The point I am making is that a condition of spiritual depression is not only bad in and of itself, it is possibly the greatest hindrance of all to the process of sanctification. This is true of us in every respect, is it not? 'The joy of the Lord,' says Nehemiah, 'is your strength' (8:10). And how true that is! I do not care what work you are doing, if you are not happy you will not do it well. If you are preoccupied with yourself, or if you have some worry or something on your mind and your spirit, it will affect all the work you do. You can never work well while there is a kind of division within you. The man who really works well is the man who is carefree and is working with joy.

A great deal of attention is being paid to this whole matter at the present time. It is one of the major problems of our so-called civilisation. Mankind is unhappy, hence all this interest in psychology. It is just being realised that if people are not happy they will not work well. All that is equally true in the spiritual life, and there is no question at all but that a doubt or uncertainty about my real standing before God, a doubt as to whether I am a Christian or not, constitutes a great hindrance to sanctification. In other words, people who are struggling to make themselves Christian can never be sanctified.

I do not hesitate for a moment to speak as strongly as that. Someone may be very pious, but there is all the difference in the world between piety and sanctification. The man who is truly sanctified is pious, but you can be pious without being sanctified. By this I mean that there are people whose whole vocation in life is to be religious. You are familiar with that, perhaps, in a highly organised form in Roman Catholicism. These people enter upon the devout life and make a distinction between the 'religious' and the 'laity'. Now we disagree with that entirely, and I am simply using it to show that these people are trying, by their efforts and exertions, to make themselves Christian.

But the New Testament teaching is that while you are trying to make yourself a Christian you will never be one, and if you are not a Christian you cannot be sanctified. The only people whom God does sanctify are his own people, those who are Christian. That is why I maintain that an assurance of one's standing before God is an essential preliminary to this process of sanctification.

So we must start with this, and the question therefore arises as to how we can arrive at this assurance. And here we must start with the great biblical doctrine of justification. 'Ah,' says someone, 'there you are. You are bringing up those old terms again. These legal terms of the apostle Paul are out of date. "Justification" – I am not interested in theology and in justification!' Well, my friend, all I say to you is that if you are not interested in justification, I can assure you that you are ignorant with regard to sanctification. Justification is an utter, absolute necessity. There is no assurance apart from being clear about the doctrine of justification. Why does Scripture tell us so much about it? Why does it expound it as it does? Is it simply to expound doctrine? Of course not! All these letters were written with a very practical object and intent. They were written to help people, to encourage and strengthen them, and to show them how to live the Christian life in ordinary affairs. And therefore this doctrine of justification is an absolute essential, for without it we shall never really assume a true Christian position and begin to enjoy its great blessings.

What, then, is the teaching? Well, the great argument of Romans is that we are 'justified freely by his grace' (Rom 3:24). This means that God declares and pronounces that you and I who believe in the Lord Jesus Christ are guiltless. Here we are – we are sinners. We have sinned, as the whole world has sinned. 'There is none righteous, no, not one.' We are not only born in sin, we have committed deliberate acts of sin. The greatest sin of all, of course, is not to live our lives entirely for God, not to glorify him as he meant us to do, and not to fulfil the purpose for which he created us. We have all

sinned before God. We have broken his laws and his commandments; we are all guilty sinners deserving nothing but
punishment and retribution.

But this is the amazing message, and this is what is meant
by justification – that God tells us that, as the result of the
work of the Lord Jesus Christ, because of his life, his death
and his resurrection, if we believe on him and trust ourselves
solely and entirely to him, God pardons and forgives our
sins. Not only that, he declares that we are free from guilt:
more than that, justification includes this. He not only
declares that we are pardoned and forgiven and that we are
guiltless, he also declares that we are positively righteous. He
imputes to us, that is, he puts to our account, the righteousness of the Lord Jesus Christ himself, who was entirely without sin, who never failed his Father in any way, and who
never broke a Commandment or transgressed any law. God
gives to us – puts upon us – the righteousness of the Lord
Jesus Christ himself, and then looks upon us and pronounces
that we are righteous in his holy sight. That is the biblical
doctrine of justification.

Now you will notice the way in which I am putting this; I
am emphasising this pronouncement of God, and I do that
very deliberately because the doctrine of justification is what
you may call a forensic or a legal statement. It is the pronouncement or the promulgation of a sentence. The picture
we should have in our minds is that of a Judge seated upon the
bench and there we are standing in the dock, charged by the
law, by Satan, and by our own consciences, but without a
plea and without an excuse. And there stands the Lord Jesus
Christ proclaiming that he lived and has died for us, and that
he has paid the penalty on our behalf. Then God the Judge
eternal pronounces that he accepts that and that therefore
from henceforth he regards us as guiltless. Our sins are all
blotted out as a thick cloud. He casts them into the sea of his
own forgetfulness, and throws them behind his back – they
are gone, and gone for ever.

Not only that, he says that he regards us in the light of this righteousness of his Son, so he pronounces us free from guilt and clothed with the righteousness of the Lord Jesus Christ. The Bible uses many analogies to bring out this idea; here is one of them. It is as if we were standing with our clothes torn almost to rags, covered and bespattered with the mud, the mire, and the filth of this world. Suddenly all that is taken from us, and we are clothed with a most gorgeous, glorious and perfect cloak, spotless in its whiteness and in its purity; the transformation is entire and the picture is altogether changed. It has all been done for us freely and for nothing.

Indeed we can put the doctrine of justification like this: if we believe on the Lord Jesus Christ and belong to him, God regards us as if we had never sinned at all. It is nothing less than that! It is actually that God in all his holiness and in the light of the law and everything else, looks down upon us, and then, having thus covered us by his Son, sees us in Christ and regards us as if we had never sinned at all. If we believe anything less than that, we are not believing the New Testament doctrine of justification by faith only: that we are justified freely by the grace of God. That is the doctrine, and I would emphasise that it is the essential preliminary to this process of sanctification which God then works in us and brings to pass in us by means of his wonderful truth. That is the argument you must derive from the work of Christ upon the cross and from the Resurrection.

But clearly that is only the essential starting-point. It is a point which we must always bear in mind, but we do not stop at that. We must go on to say that not only are we thus declared to be righteous in a forensic or a legal manner, but that we are actually in union with Christ and joined to him. You cannot have read the New Testament even cursorily without noticing this constantly repeated phrase – 'in Christ' – 'in Christ Jesus'. The apostles go on repeating it and it is one of the most significant and glorious statements in the entire realm and range of truth. It means that we are joined to the Lord Jesus Christ; we have become a part of him. We are in him. We belong to him. We are members of his body.

And the teaching is that God regards us as such; and this, of course, means that now, in this relationship, we are sharers in, and partakers of, everything that is true of the Lord Jesus Christ himself. In other words, our standing before God is not only a legal one – it is a legal one, and we must start with that – but we go beyond the legal standing to this vital fact that our position is in Christ.

Now we must watch the apostle working that out in Romans 6. The first thing that is true of us, he says, is that we have died with Christ and have been buried with him. 'Shall we continue in sin, that grace may abound? God forbid!' Why? Because 'How shall we, that are dead to sin, live any longer therein?' (vv. 1–2).

'But,' one might ask, 'what do you mean by saying that I am dead to sin? I am in the flesh and I am still the same person, and I am still in the same world. What do you mean by saying that I am dead to sin? I am still being tempted, I still sometimes fall. How do you mean I am dead to sin?' But, read on. 'Know ye not,' says Paul, 'that so many of us as were baptized into Jesus Christ, were baptized into his death? Therefore we are buried with him by baptism into death: that like as Christ was raised up from the dead ... even so we also should walk in newness of life. For if we have been planted together in the likeness of his death' – if that is true – 'we shall be also in the likeness of his resurrection' (vv. 3–5).

Paul goes on repeating that truth and working it out. But are we clear about this? Do we realise that as Christians we must make these assertions about ourselves? As we saw, the first assertion which I must make is that because I am joined to the Lord Jesus Christ and am part of him, everything that is true of him is true of me, and therefore the first thing which is at once true of me is that everything that happened to him in his death has happened to me also. That is the argument – I am in Christ.

It is important that we do not take this chapter on its own, but along with the previous chapter. There the great statement has been that we were all in Adam. And so we sinned in

Adam. Everything that Adam did has been imputed to us and has become true of us. In exactly the same way, everything that is true of Christ is true of us because it is all imputed to us. And this is the first thing: the Lord Jesus Christ was made of a woman, made under the law. He lived his life in this world under the law of God. The law made its demands upon him, and if he had broken any of it, he would have suffered the consequences. But he kept it perfectly. Not only that; he died under the law. He took the sins of men, who had been condemned by the law, upon himself, and for them he died, under the law and to the law.

So henceforward the law has nothing to say to him, or to do with him. He has died to the law once, and what Paul says is that that is equally true of me. He says that as a Christian, as one who is in Christ, I have finished with the law, it has nothing to do with me and I am dead to it. Paul goes on to work that out in Romans 7 in his figure of the married relationship. He says that the Christian was once like a married woman who was bound to her husband while he was alive. But when the husband died she was no longer bound to him and she was free to marry again. He says that that was exactly our position; we were once married to the law, but that is finished with, and we are therefore married to another, even to Christ. That is why we all, as Christians, should be able to sing the words of Augustus Toplady's hymn:

> The terrors of law and of God
> With me can have nothing to do;
> My Saviour's obedience and blood
> Hide all my transgressions from view.

'There is therefore now no condemnation to them which are in Christ Jesus' (Rom 8:1) – none. From the standpoint of salvation, we are dead to the law; we are finished with it.

Not only that, Paul says, we are equally dead to the dominion of Satan. He works that out here – 'Sin shall not have dominion over you' (Rom 6:14). You are not any longer under the dominion of sin. We have been translated out of the kingdom of darkness into the kingdom of God's dear Son. We are taken out of the whole realm over which Satan rules; we are dead to that.

This again is a very vital aspect of the truth in its practical application. 'The whole world,' says the apostle John, in his first epistle, 'lieth in wickedness' – but we do not; 'and that wicked one toucheth us not' (1 Jn 5:19, 18). He cannot touch us. We do not belong to the kingdom of Satan; we belong to the kingdom of the Lord Jesus Christ. Satan is governing and ruling and controlling and dominating the lives of all who do not belong to Christ. Whether they know it or not, it is an absolute fact. He is just gripping them and controlling them utterly and absolutely. They cannot move without him. But a Christian is one who has been taken out of that and put into this other kingdom. He has finished with the dominion of Satan.

'Ah yes,' you may say, 'but we still sin, and Satan can still get us down.' Yes, but not because you are in his dominion, but rather because you are foolish enough, having been taken out of his dominion, still to listen to him. He has no authority over you, no power at all, and if you yield to him it is entirely due to your own folly. We are dead to Satan as well as dead to the law, and we are equally dead to sin. 'How shall we,' Paul asks, 'that are dead to sin, live any longer therein?' Here he means dead to the dominion of sin, and he puts that in a positive form by saying, 'Sin shall not have dominion over you.' You may fall to temptation, but that does not mean that it has dominion over you. Your life is no longer controlled by the sinful outlook. You are not living in the realm of sin. You are not 'continuing in sin' as John puts it in l John 3. We are dead to all that.

Yes, but we must go even further: the Christian is one who is even dead to his old self, to his old nature, to that condition which he inherited from Adam. We are all born with this Adamic nature, governed by passion and lust and desire and controlled by the way of the world. I need not keep you about this: we are all perfectly familiar with it. The tragedy with men and women who boast about their freedom because they are not Christians, is that they are utter and absolute slaves to the way of the world. Look at the poor creatures as you see them depicted so constantly in the newspapers, all doing the same thing, rushing about like sheep. They never think; they are simply carried away by what is being done. That is the serfdom of this old Adamic nature. If we are Christians we are no longer like that; we are dead to it all. We are dead to that old self, to that old life. We have been given a new nature. We have finished with the old self once and for all. We are now in Christ. We have a new life and a new outlook. 'Old things are passed away; behold, all things are become new' (2 Cor 5:17).

So let me put it very plainly in this way: there is no point in our saying that we believe that Christ has died for us, and that we believe our sins are forgiven, unless we can also say that for us old things are passed away and that all things are become new; that our outlook towards the world and its method of living is entirely changed. It is not that we are sinless, nor that we are perfect, but that we have finished with that way of life. We have seen it for what it is, and we are new creatures for whom everything has become new.

But I can imagine somebody saying, 'Don't you think that this is rather a dangerous doctrine? Don't you think it is dangerous to tell people that they are dead to sin, dead to the law, dead to Satan, and that God regards them as if they had never sinned at all? Won't the effect of that make such people say, "All right, in view of that, it does not matter what I do"?' But Paul says that what happens is the exact opposite, and that must be so because to be saved and to be truly Christian means that we are in Christ, and if we are in Christ, we are dead to sin, dead to Satan, dead to the world, dead to our old selves: we are like our Lord.

Let me put that positively. We have not only died with Christ, we have also risen with him: 'Therefore we are buried with him by baptism into death: that like as Christ was raised up from the dead by the glory of the Father, even so we also should walk in newness of life' (Rom 6:4). So you do not say at a meeting, 'Yes, I believe in Christ, I accept forgiveness,' and then go back and live exactly as you lived before. Not at all! We live in 'newness of life'. We have been raised with Christ. Notice Paul's logical way of putting this – he says, '... reckon ye also yourselves to be dead indeed unto sin, but alive unto God through Jesus Christ our Lord' (v. 11). For before we were not alive unto God, but were dead in trespasses and sins. Oh yes, we prayed when we were in trouble, we perhaps said our prayers once a day, but we were not alive unto God.

But when we become alive to God, it means that he is at the centre of our lives; God is a living reality to us. God is not just a term, not just some mechanical agency to dispense blessings to us. God is a person, whom we now know. 'This is life eternal,' as our Lord has already reminded us, 'that they might know thee the only true God, and Jesus Christ, whom thou hast sent.' We are alive unto God. He is real; he is living; we have fellowship with him. And when we pray we do not just utter some thoughts, and hope they will do us good, we know that we are speaking to God, that we are in his presence and that he speaks to us. It is a living fellowship.

More than that, in Christ we are not only alive to God, we have become children of God. He is the Son of God, and all who are in him are therefore God's children. We receive his life; the very life of God himself has entered into us and into our souls, and thus we are living a new type of life altogether – a living life in the presence of the living God.

John's dictum is that the Christian is one who goes through this world realising that he is 'walking with God'. It is a great walk, a companionship. You journey through life, through the darkness of this world, in the light of the presence of God. That is what it means to be a Christian; hating sin and evil and everything that tends to separate us from God. If you should for a moment turn away and fall, then you go back to him and confess your sin, and we know that 'he is faithful and just to forgive us our sins, and to cleanse us from all unrighteousness' (1 Jn 5:9). Yes, but that does not just lead us to sin again: no, we have learned to hate that, and we hate ourselves for having looked at it, instead of always looking to him. We do not want what is wrong, but rather to be alive unto God in a living, loving fellowship, walking with him through this life and all its temptations and all its sin and shame; dead to sin with him; buried with him; risen and alive with him; in him; partaking of his life; a child of God.

And the last thing which is emphasised is that we have not only died with Christ, but that even at this moment we are seated with him in the heavenly places. We are far away, above all principality, might and dominion, and every power that can be named, because being in Christ means that what is true of him, is true of us. That is what you are, says the New Testament.

As we consider this, I think we see that it is obviously the profoundest doctrine we can ever contemplate. Is there anything that is more encouraging, more uplifting, than to know that all this is true of us? That is what Paul is telling these Romans; that is what the other New Testament writers are constantly stressing. We must cease to think of ourselves only in terms of the forgiveness of sins. We must never isolate that, and leave it on its own. The Christian is one; his life is a whole and indivisible. As truth is one, he is one, and he is one with Christ; and if he is a Christian at all, all these things must be true of him. It is because these things are true, that God forgives us, and regards us as justified. That is the truth about us – the whole, wonderful truth – that I am dead even to the law of God. There is now no condemnation. I am dead to sin, dead to Satan; right outside their territory, outside their dominion altogether. I am alive to God, his child, a partaker of the divine nature, and in a living fellowship and communion with God. That is the doctrine, that is the argument.

But see the deduction: if all that is true, how can we continue in sin? Why do we even want to? The very fact that we want to should make us wonder whether we are Christians at all. It is impossible if this is true of us and if we realise this. Therefore Paul brings out his great deductions at the end: 'But God be thanked, that ye were the servants of sin, but ye have obeyed from the heart that form of doctrine which was delivered you. Being then made free from sin, ye became the servants [the bond-slaves] of righteousness' (Rom 6:17–18). As you wanted to do one thing, you now want to do this other. As you were a slave to that, you are now a slave to this.

Then he says, 'I speak after the manner of men because of the infirmity of your flesh ...' (v. 19). He is going to use an illustration and he apologises for doing so. He says, You force me to do it because you are so slow to understand: '... for as ye have yielded your members servants to uncleanness, and to iniquity unto iniquity; even so now yield your members servants to righteousness unto holiness.'

In other words, he says, because of this entire change in your position, take your very faculties and powers, your enthusiasm, your joy, your happiness, take all the thrills that you used to get in that old life and turn them into this new direction. Let me put it as simply as the apostle does, and even more simply, almost in a childish manner. If you want to know whether you are a true Christian according to Romans 6, you can put it like this: Do you get the same thrill out of your Christian life as you used to get out of that old life? Does a prayer meeting thrill you now as much as a cinema used to? That is his argument. Your 'members' that used to be given as 'servants to uncleanness and to iniquity unto inquity', must now be 'servants to righteousness unto holiness'.

Let me use the modern jargon – you got a great kick out of that old life did you not? Are you getting a kick out of your Christian life? Do you find it exciting? Do you find it thrilling? Do you find it wonderful? Do you find yourself at times almost beside yourself with joy? Is it bubbling over from within? As you used to speak, going home in the underground or in the bus, after you had seen a play or something like that, and you were so animated and excited,

do you ever speak like that about the word of God and
about fellowship with the saints, and about praying to God,
and the contemplation of eternity? That is the argument –
you were that, you are now this. As that was true, so this
must now be true. And as we understand something of all
this, and begin to apply it and to practise it, God's marvellous process of sanctification will be going on in us.

I have reminded you every time, from the very beginning, that sanctification means being separated unto God. It
means being prepared for heaven and the vision of God and
glory eternal. There is not much time to be lost, my friends.
We are here today and gone tomorrow. The end of all
things may be at hand – I do not know. But I do know this,
that if I really believe I am going to him to spend my eternity with him, then the sooner I leave these other things the
better. They keep me from him. They are unlike him, and
if I do not know what it is to enjoy God here in this life and
in this world, then it seems to me that heaven will be the
most boring place imaginable for me: my heaven will
become hell. The truth is, of course, that in that case I shall
never get there, because I have never belonged to him. Let
us examine ourselves to make sure that we really believe in
Christ and his work on our behalf. It leads to all this – we
have died with him, we have risen with him. We are alive to
God, children of God. We are new creatures. Oh, beloved
Christians, let the whole world know that this is true of us!

# 10

## *Christ in Us*

*Sanctify them through thy truth: thy word is truth (v. 17).*

We saw in our last study how nothing so promotes sanctification as the realisation that we are in Christ; the realisation that we are declared righteous by God, that we are justified, and that God looks upon us now as in Christ. So here we are, then, people in Christ facing a new life, the kind of life that he lived, and we realise now that we are called to live in that way. John puts it in his first epistle like this: 'As he is, so are we in this world' (1 Jn 4:17). We are to follow in his steps who did no wrong: '... neither was guile found in his mouth: who, when he was reviled, reviled not again; when he suffered, he threatened not; but committed himself to him that judgeth righteously' (1 Pet 2:22–23). That is what is meant by being sanctified – we are to be like him. Sanctification is not so much an experience, as to be like him; to be separated from the world and sin; to be separated unto God. This is the whole process of the teaching; being in Christ, we are called to live even as he lived in this world.

But then, I imagine someone saying at this point, 'How can this be done? Who are we that we should even attempt to live such a life?' And that brings us to the next aspect of the truth that we must consider, for we are told very plainly in the Scriptures that we are not left to ourselves. God does not call us to an impossible life, and command us to live it, and then leave us to ourselves to do so somehow, anyhow. That is an entirely false

125

understanding of the scriptural teaching, for here we come to this next great emphasis, which is that the Christian is one who is regenerated. All the ethical teaching of the Scriptures is based upon that supposition. All the appeals made in the epistles for conduct and behaviour – and we must never be tired of pointing this out – are always made to Christian people.

It is a fatal thing to expect Christian conduct from people who are not Christians. The Bible never asks that. The Bible knows that the natural man, the man born with human nature as it has been since the fall of Adam, cannot possibly live such a life. The whole point of the giving of the Ten Commandments under the moral law is, in a sense, just to prove that. As Paul argues in the epistle to the Romans, the law was added 'that sin by the commandment might become exceeding sinful' (Rom 7:13). God did not give the law to the Children of Israel in the hope that possibly they might keep it and thereby save themselves. That was impossible. It could not be done. The 'carnal mind is enmity against God, for it is not subject to the law of God, neither indeed can be' (Rom 8:7). So the law was given in order, to use a modern phrase, to pinpoint sin, to bring home to us our sinfulness; to establish our guilt; to show us our utter helplessness.

Furthermore, if it is impossible for man, as he is by nature, to keep the moral law as given by God to man through Moses, how much more impossible is it for any man, in his own strength or power, to live the kind of life that the Lord Jesus Christ lived, or to live the Sermon on the Mount. It is utterly and absolutely impossible. On the contrary, let me say it again, all the ethical and moral appeals in the New Testament are always based on the assumption that the people to whom they are addressed are Christians; that they are regenerated; that they have undergone what is called a 'new birth'.

This is great and vital teaching. We could very easily occupy ourselves for some time with this, but I do not propose to do that now. I am simply indicating here the big principles which we can work out for ourselves, and at this point I am concerned only with the doctrine of regeneration or rebirth as it has this very practical bearing upon the process of sanctification. My argument is that it is only as we know ourselves to be new men and women in Christ Jesus, that we really can be sanctified. Now that is the kind of terminology which you find so freely in the New Testament. We are told that we have become 'partakers of the divine nature', so that, as we confront this great task of following Christ, of living in the world the kind of life that he lived when he himself was here, we have no excuse. We must not say, 'Oh, but who am I? I am so weak and so frail!' The Scripture comes at once and says, 'But you are born again; you are a new creature. You have been created anew. You are a partaker of the divine nature. You are not simply a natural man, there is a new man in you.' And it is in the light of this that it presses its great teaching about sanctification.

Without going into this in detail, let me summarise it by putting it in this way. The teaching in the Scripture is that there is a new principle of life in us and that God, by the work of the Holy Spirit, has implanted this new principle in us. It is not something substantial – no new substance has been injected into us. There is, however, very definitely, a new principle at work in us which leads to a new disposition, and its effect is that we are now made capable of doing things that we were not capable of doing before.

It starts, of course, by giving us an entirely new view of everything: '... if any man be in Christ, he is a new creature: old things are passed away; behold, all things are become new' (2 Cor 5:17). Or take it as our Lord put it to Nicodemus in the famous interview in John 3. Nicodemus was trying to understand, and he was obviously about to put a whole series of questions which might help him to grasp what our Lord was saying. But Christ stops him and says, 'Verily, verily, I say unto thee. Except a man be born again, he cannot see the kingdom of God ... Except a man be born of water and of the Spirit, he cannot enter into the kingdom of God. That which is born of the flesh is flesh; and that which is born of the Spirit is spirit' (Jn 3:3, 5, 6).

Our Lord is saying, Nicodemus, you must not try to understand. You need this new principle, this new life, this new power, this something must happen to you which is comparable to the effect of the wind – '... thou hearest the sound thereof, but canst not tell whence it cometh, and whither it goeth: so is every one that is born of the Spirit' (v. 8). It is a supernatural operation of the Spirit of God upon the soul of man, and a man finds himself different. He is a new creature, a new creation, and he has a new outlook, and a new attitude towards everything.

So it is obvious, surely, that this is a most potent influence in the matter of our sanctification, for when a man is born again he has an entirely new view of God. The trouble with the natural man is that his view of God is wrong. He is 'at enmity against God'; an enemy and an alien in his mind, says Paul. He is outside the 'commonwealth' of Israel, 'without God in the world' (Eph 2:12). That is the difficulty with the man who is not in Christ, he is a God hater. Even when he claims that he believes in God, he really hates him. He does not know God and his ideas concerning him are all wrong. What the devil did to man was to insinuate a false view of God which has persisted ever since. But when we are given this new nature and when the new principle comes in, we have the right view of God for the first time; and obviously we can never be sanctified until this happens to us.

Then we also have a new view of God's law. The law of God is no longer grievous to the Christian. '... his commandments,' says John, 'are not grievous' (1 Jn 5:3). Christians love God's law. They know that it is right and true. It does not go against the grain for them because now their whole attitude is changed. This is an essential part of their sanctification. Formerly they looked at the law and saw that it was against them. They wished that it was not there. But now they love it; they delight in it; they want it; they want to be conformed to it. The whole position is changed.

And in the same way they have an entirely different view of sin. Those who are born again hate sin. They bemoan the fact that there is any sinful principle still left in them. They know something about the experience of Romans 7. Have you been there? Have you been in Romans 7? Have you ever known what t is to hate the sin that is in you – this principle, this law in your members? Have you ever felt desperate about yourself? Have you ever cried out, 'Oh wretched man that I am! who shall deliver me from the body of this death?' People who are born again inevitably know something about that experience. They cannot help it; they must know it. Sin has become abhorrent to them – hateful – because it is unlike God. It is the greatest enemy of their souls.

In the same way, of course, the Christian's whole view of Christ is changed. Only the one who has been born again truly knows the Lord Jesus Christ. The princes of this world do not known him; it was they who crucified him, says Paul. And they did so because they did not know the Lord of Glory: if they had known him they would never have done it. It is only the Holy Spirit who can enable a person truly to understand and to know the Lord Jesus Christ. That is why we should never be surprised that very able, intelligent people do not believe the gospel. They cannot. 'The natural man receiveth not the things of the Spirit of God ... neither can he know them, because they are spiritually discerned' (1 Cor 2:14). We need the 'mind of Christ', and in the regeneration, we have the mind of Christ.

And thus, the New Testament tells us, the Christian is entirely new and entirely changed, and he hungers and thirsts after righteousness. Now at the very minimum, regeneration means that, and you cannot be a Christian without that having happened to you. That is what makes us Christian – that God has worked this mighty operation upon us, and has implanted in us this new principle of life. As that other principle came in at the Fall, so this new principle now comes in, and it changes our entire outlook. But I must leave it at that and go on to what is, in a sense, another aspect of the same great truth.

We were emphasising earlier the fact that, as Christians, we are in Christ. I am anxious to emphasise now that it is equally true that Christ is in us. There are two sides to this. We have seen that we are united to Christ, and that therefore all he has done we have done. But it is also true to say that he is in us. You notice if you read John 14, 15 and 16 – the introduction, if you like, to this great prayer – that our Lord keeps on saying, 'I in you, and you in me.' 'The Father in me, and I in the Father.' That is his language. We are in him and he is in us, and this emphasis, this aspect of the truth, is as vital in the matter of our sanctification as is the other truth which emphasises that we are in him.

There is great teaching about this everywhere in the Scriptures. I again commend to you those three chapters in John; but you will find it richly in all the New Testament epistles, and in particular, perhaps, in the epistles of the apostle Paul. Let me just quote to you at random some of the leading statements. In Romans 8:10 he puts it like this: 'And if Christ be in you, the body is dead because of sin; but the Spirit is life because of righteousness.' But you notice the statement – 'if Christ be in you'. Paul's argument is that if he is not in you, you are not a Christian: but if you are a Christian, then he is in you.

Or take 2 Corinthians 13:5: 'Know ye not your own selves, how that Jesus Christ is in you, except ye be reprobates?' What a tremendous statement! Then of course, there is the great statement in Galatians 2:20: 'I live, yet not I, but Christ liveth in me: and the life which I now live in the flesh I live by the faith of the Son of God, who loved me and gave himself for me.' Again in Ephesians 3:17 Paul prays for the Ephesians: 'That Christ may dwell in your hearts by faith.' Then listen to him in that great triumphant statement in Colossians 1:27: 'To whom,' he says, 'God would make known what is the riches of the glory of this mystery among the Gentiles; which is Christ in you, the hope of glory.' And again in the same epistle, in 3:4, he says, 'When Christ, who is our life, shall appear, then shall ye also appear with him in glory.' He is our life now, and he is going to appear.

I have simply taken some of these great statements at random, but you notice that they all unite in saying that if we are Christians, the simple truth is that Christ is in us. Not only am I united to Christ indissolubly and am a sharer, therefore, of all that is true of him, but Christ is in me. He turned to those disciples, who were crestfallen and heartbroken when he told them that he was about to leave them, and said, Do not worry, do not let sorrow fill your hearts. 'Let not your heart be troubled: ye believe in God, believe also in me' (Jn 14:1). He said, Do you know, it is a good thing for you that I am going. As it is now, I am with you, but I am outside you. My going will mean that I shall not only be with you but that I shall be *in* you: I am going to take up my abode in you. The Father and I will take up our abode in you through the Holy Spirit. We are going to send the Holy Spirit, and in him we will come and reside – take up our residence, dwell – within you. 'It is expedient for you that I go away: for if I go not away, the Comforter will not come unto you; but if I depart, I will send him unto you' (Jn 16:7). That is the argument.

Christian people, is it not obvious to us all that we are living very, very much below the position which we are meant to be in? Do you realise that Christ is in you, that Christ is in your heart by faith? What is the thing we preach? asks Paul, writing to the Colossians, who, remember, were Gentiles. He says, This is the mystery, this is the marvellous mystic message, the astounding thing that has been committed to me and to the other preachers of the gospel – 'Christ in you, the hope of glory' (Col 1:27). What hope have I of glory? It is that Christ is in me; Christ dwelling in our hearts by faith.

I wonder whether we can appropriate the language of the apostle Paul, and whether we can say, honestly and truly, 'I live, yet not I but Christ liveth in me'? My friends, the Lord Jesus Christ came into the world and endured all he did, and went to that agony and the shame of the cross, in order that you and I might be able to say that. You notice that I am dealing with this doctrine only from the standpoint of sanctification. It is a doctrine that can be worked out on many other lines, but we are concerned in particular about the truth that sanctifies – 'Sanctify them in [or through] thy truth: thy word is truth' – and here is an aspect of it. 'How can I live a sanctified holy life?' you ask. The answer is, Christ is in you, living his life in you. Let nobody try to say that this is a truth about certain special Christians: it is true of all Christians. The apostle Paul not only says this about himself, he presses this upon all others. His prayer for the Ephesians is that they may be 'strengthened with might by his Spirit in the inner man' and that 'Christ may dwell in their hearts by faith', and so on.

Therefore, as we look at this great truth it seems to me that one of the first things we must lay hold of is the solemn and simple fact that if we are believers at all in the Lord Jesus Christ, we are in him and he is also in us. This means that as you wake up in the morning and consider the kind of life you are expected to live, as you realise the sinfulness of the world in which you walk, as you know something of the attacks of the devil, the principalities and powers, the rulers of the darkness of this world, the spiritual wickedness in the high places which are set against you, you must put up, against all that, your shield of faith, by which you say, 'Yes, that is all true, but Christ is in me. I am not alone, because he dwells in me.' And you live by that faith, and you go on and you conquer and you prevail.

Now, let me divide that up a little by showing how this works. And I suggest that the first thing we must do is to realise this truth. Notice how our Lord has put it in John 6:53: 'Except ye eat the flesh of the Son of man, and drink his blood, ye have no life in you.' But then he goes on to say, 'Whoso eateth my flesh, and drinketh my blood, hath eternal life; and I will raise him up at the last day. For my flesh is meat indeed, and my blood is drink indeed' (vv. 54–55). Then he repeats it all – 'He that eateth my flesh, and drinketh my blood, dwelleth in me, and I in him. As the living Father hath sent me, and I live by the Father: so he that eateth me, even he shall live by me. This is that bread which came down from heaven ... he that eateth of this bread shall live for ever' (vv. 56–58).

The argument is perfectly plain and simple. What you and I need in order to be able to live this sanctified, holy Christian life, is spiritual life, energy and power. Where can I get these things? Our Lord tells us that there is only one way: we must 'eat his flesh and drink his blood'. Is that a reference to taking communion regularly? Not at all! 'The words that I speak unto you,' he says in verse 63, 'they are spirit and they are life.' No, he means that we realise that he is in us, and that, as it were, as we partake of our food and drink, so we shall partake of him spiritually. He is speaking in a spiritual sense, not of something material. No grace can be infused by baptism, or be received in bread or wine, it comes by a spiritual partaking of him. The people asked materially, 'How can we eat of his flesh?'

You do not understand, he says, you will always materialise everything; you are carnal in your outlook. My words, 'they are spirit and they are life', understand them spiritually.

In verse 57 of the same chapter it is made very clear. He says, 'As the living Father hath sent me and I live by the Father: so he that eateth me, even he shall live by me.' How did he take of the living Father? Did he eat bread and drink wine? No, of course not: he partook of his Father spiritually, and we are to partake of him in exactly the same way.

To do so means meditating upon him; thinking about him; realising these truths; masticating them, as it were; dwelling upon them; taking them into ourselves; saying by faith, 'Yes, I believe the word, Christ is in me, and I am going to partake of him.' But not only that. We must not only live by him in the sense I have just been describing; we must go to him constantly and take of his fullness. John puts it in the prologue of this Gospel when he says, 'And of his fulness have all we received, and grace for grace' (Jn 1:16). What he means is, I am living by him, I go to him for everything. In him are treasures for ever more, the treasures of grace and of wisdom and of goodness. God has put all this in Christ, and all I must do is to go to Christ and I receive it.

Now this is a very practical matter. We find our Lord constantly saying it throughout this Gospel of John. For example, in chapter 7:37, he cries: 'If any man thirst, let him come unto me, and drink.' And remember that 'come' here has the sense of 'keep on coming', so what he says is: 'If any man thirst, let him keep on coming unto me to drink.' Let us be very practical here; it is as simple as this. If you find yourself at some time, at any point in your life in this world, tired, weary, not only physically, but mentally, and perhaps still more, spiritually, what do you do about it? Well, he tells you to go to him! He is in you, dwelling in you. Go to him as you would go to a fountain or a tap to draw water – go to Christ. Tell him about your thirst and your weakness, your lethargy and your helplessness, and ask him to give you life-giving water, to give you this heavenly bread: to give you himself. He is pledged to do that, but we only know it for ourselves as we realise that he is in us, and as we turn to him and go to him.

He puts it like this, in effect, when he turns to the disciples who are troubled about his leaving them, and says, 'You are so unhappy because of a weakness in your thinking. You say, "Whenever we have been in trouble we have just gone straight to him and asked him a question, and he has always been able to answer it. He has given us power to cast out devils, and to speak to people, but if he is going away, what shall we do?"' His answer is this: 'It is going to be better, because, though I am going away, I am coming back and I am going to be *in* you: I will always be in you. You simply turn to me and I will give you all you need.' So we must draw 'of his fulness'. Indeed, I am not going too far when I put it like this: the New Testament tells us that there is no excuse for failure in the Christian. If we fail it is because we are not taking of his fullness and the promised grace upon grace.

Let me repeat that in another way: we must realise his strength and his power. He has already been emphasising that in the fifteenth chapter. He has compared us, in our relationship to him, to branches in the vine, and he has said categorically that 'without me ye can do nothing', nothing at all (Jn 15:5). A branch can do nothing except in its relationship to the trunk, the parent tree and we are exactly like that. But what power there is in the tree! Take Paul's prayer for the people at Ephesus, in Ephesians 1. Paul prays that the 'eyes of your understanding [may be] enlightened that ye may know …', and he goes on to request three main things. I am emphasising the third here, and it is this: 'What is the exceeding greatness of his power to us-ward who believe, according to the working of his mighty power, which he wrought in Christ, when he raised him from the dead' (v. 19). *That* is the power that is working in us as Christians; that is the power that is working in us now. The power that raised Christ from the dead is now working in us mightily in our sanctification. Or consider again the apostle Paul's great doxology at the end of Ephesians 3: 'Now unto him that is able to do exceeding abundantly above all that we can ask or think, according to the power that worketh in us.' This is not in the apostles only, but in *all* Christians. That is the power – 'exceeding abundantly above all that we can ask or think'. Or hear him as he writes to the Colossians. He says that he is preaching the gospel, 'Whereunto I also labour, striving according to his working, which worketh in me mightily' (Col 1:29); the power of God in Christ through the Holy Spirit.

That, then, is the way in which we become sanctified and live the sanctified life. We must stop talking about our weakness: we must take more of his power! We must realise that Christ is in us with all this power: that the power that enabled him to resist the temptations of the devil is the power that is in us.

Lastly, I would put it like this – and sometimes I think it is the most effective argument of all. The truth about Christ dwelling in me promotes my sanctification by giving me an entirely new view of sin. I find so often, when people come to discuss with me this problem of sin, that all along they are tending to think of sin in terms of this or that particular sin that gets them down. This doctrine we are looking at gives us a new view of it, it makes you look at it like this: What is sin? Well, sin is not so much something that I do or that I should not do: sin is that which separates me from God. He is in me, dwelling in me, and my life is meant to be a life of communion and of fellowship with him. Sin is allowing myself, even for a single moment, to turn away from him.

Imagine yourself having audience with the Queen or somebody whom you regard as great in this world. What would she say if, instead of looking at her and listening to what she was saying, you were looking at someone else or gazing out of the window, patently thinking about something else? She would feel insulted, and rightly so. Nothing is more insulting than not looking at the person talking to you and not listening to what is being said. The New Testament tells me that Christ is in me, and I am meant to live a life of constant fellowship and communion with him. Sin is to look away from him; to be interested in anything that the world can give rather than in him. Oh, if it is something foul it is ten times worse; but the best that the world has got to give me is an insult to him, if I put it before him.

There are endless statements of this; Paul puts it in terms of the Holy Spirit, 'Know ye not that your body is the temple of the Holy Ghost which is in you?' (1 Cor 6:19). The argument is about fornication and adultery. Paul does not give a moral lecture on immorality; he says in effect, 'What is wrong about that, is that you are joining your body, which is a temple of the Holy Spirit, to another, and you have no right to do it. The way to overcome that sin is not to pray so much that you may be delivered from it; it is to realise that your body is the temple of the Holy Spirit, and that you have no right to use it in that way.' Another way he puts it is this, and it is very tender: 'Grieve not the Holy Spirit of God' (Eph 4:30). He is tender, he is sensitive, he is holy; do not grieve him.

And if you and I would only think of our lives like that, it would very soon begin to promote our sanctification. May I again commend to you that simple morning rule. When you wake up, the first thing you should do (and I too need to do the same) is say to yourself, 'I am a child of God. Christ is in me. That old self is gone: I died with Christ. "I live; yet not I, but Christ liveth in me." Everything I do today, everything I think and say, must be in the light of this knowledge.' Keep him, my dear friends, in the very front of your mind and heart. Eat his flesh and drink his blood. Be constantly living on him and dwelling on him. The world will do its utmost to prevent you. 'This is the victory that overcometh the world, even our faith' (1 Jn 5:4). That means that we should realise constantly that he is in us, dwelling in our hearts by faith, and that all that we do is done as in his presence and under his holy eye. We are in Christ.

Yes, but Christ is also in us, and as we realise it we shall cast away depression and fear of the devil. We shall realise that we are not only living like him, but living with him, for him, and living by means of his power which worketh in us mightily.

What a wondrous truth is this truth by which God produces
our sanctification!

# 11

## The Doctrine of the Resurrection

*Sanctify them through thy truth: thy word is truth (v. 17).*
*Be not deceived: evil communications corrupt good manners*
*(1 Cor 15:33).*

As we continue with our consideration of this great verse –
'Father, sanctify them through thy truth [or in thy truth], thy
word is truth' – I should like to link with it the statement out of
the mighty fifteenth chapter of the first epistle to the Corinthians: 'Be not deceived: evil communications corrupt good manners' (1 Cor 15:33). In other words, I want to consider with you
the relevance of the doctrine of the Resurrection to the whole
question of our sanctification, and I propose to do so by considering the essential message of this particular chapter. Every
aspect of Christian truth, every aspect of the gospel, should
influence us and thereby promote our sanctification. We have
already looked at a number of doctrines that do this, and now
we are to consider how the particular doctrine or emphasis on
the truth of the fact of the Resurrection has a vital bearing upon
our growth in grace and our sanctification.

Now 1 Corinthians 15 is generally regarded as the great chapter on the Resurrection, and so of course it is. But there is always
the danger, it seems to me, that unless we are very careful and
consider it in its context we will not entirely understand its point
and purport. The context is always important and it is exception-
ally so in connection with this particular chapter, because it is not

138

merely a general statement of the doctrine of the Resurrection. It is that, but it is not primarily that. It was not even written for that purpose. The apostle did not sit down and say, 'Well now, it would be a good thing for me to write to the people at Corinth an account of this doctrine, and of this vital fact of the Resurrection.' There was no need for he had already done that on his first visit to Corinth with his great message.

He tells us here what he did preach to them: 'For I delivered unto you first of all that which I also received, how that Christ died for our sins according to the scriptures; and that he was buried, and that he rose again the third day, according to the scriptures: and that he was seen of Cephas, then of the twelve ...' and so on. He had already preached the facts and the interpretation and the significance and the meaning of the facts. So at this point, he was not just setting out to write an account, or make a statement of the doctrine of the Resurrection.

Neither must we regard this great chapter, as I am afraid so many tend to do, merely as a very appropriate chapter to read at a funeral. We all probably know this chapter very well for that reason. It is the custom to do this, and I am sure there are large numbers of people who instinctively think of it only in terms of a funeral – as something which is meant to give comfort and solace to the relatives of the one who is being buried. That is the context into which we tend to put it, but, as I want to show you, all that is entirely wrong. This chapter, indeed the whole epistle, was written with a very practical end in view.

The first letter to the Corinthians was not written primarily as a sort of theological treatise. There is a great deal of theology in it, as I am going to show you, but when the apostle wrote it, he was not setting out merely to write a series of statements on doctrine. Nor was it meant to be some sort of compendium of doctrine of all the letters he ever wrote. In many ways it is the most practical of his letters. It is one of those great omnibus epistles in which Paul takes up a number of questions, most of which had been sent to him by the members of the church at Corinth, or else had arisen out of certain things he had heard about some of the Christians there. If he ever sat down to write a very practical, pastoral letter, the apostle Paul did so when he wrote this one.

Paul had become very concerned about the life of the members of the church at Corinth, and, in particular, he was concerned about their behaviour. In other words, he was concerned about their sanctification. Things were happening there which were quite wrong. For instance, there was the abuse of the Communion Service, with some people eating too much and drinking too much. There was also trouble about the weaker brother, about meats offered to idols, and about the whole question of sects and divisions and schism. Now the apostle was concerned about these matters, not only from a primary theological standpoint, but particularly because of their effect upon the daily life of the church, and the life of its members.

And in exactly the same way he was concerned for them over this question of Resurrection, because certain people had been teaching them a false doctrine about it. They had been saying that it was not a fact and that there was not to be a general resurrection at all, but that resurrection was some kind of spiritual continuation of life. They were evacuating the whole idea of the Resurrection of our Lord of its true meaning and significance, and the apostle was very concerned about this. And why? Because 'evil communications corrupt good manners'. You cannot believe a wrong thing and still live a right life, says Paul. Your conduct is determined by what you believe, so evil communications, evil teachings, evil beliefs, are going to corrupt your conduct. He could see quite clearly that if this false teaching concerning the Resurrection really got a grip on these people at Corinth, then their whole life and conduct, their morality and behaviour were going to deteriorate. He declares that there is nothing, therefore, which is more vital and more urgent than that they should be right about this particular matter.

Let me translate all this into modern terms. According to the apostle Paul here, there is nothing which is quite so dangerous as to say that it does not matter very much what a man believes so long as he somehow believes in Christ; that you must not particularise over these things, and insist upon believing this or that, in detail, about these great matters. According to the apostle, that is about the most dangerous statement a person can ever make. To Paul this is so vital that he writes this powerful chapter about it.

It is important for this reason: the people who had been teaching this false doctrine regarded themselves as Christians. If they had gone to the church at Corinth and said that Christianity was all wrong and that they did not believe in Christ at all, nobody would have listened to them. But they did not do that. They purported to be Christians; they said they were preaching Christ. Yes, but they had denied his literal physical resurrection, and they still called themselves Christians. And the members of the church at Corinth who had been listening to this false teaching, and who were ready to accept it, were also members of the church, and regarded themselves as Christians. They never imagined for a moment that by believing this false doctrine they were ceasing to be Christian; they even thought it was an improvement upon the doctrine that Paul had taught them.

We begin, therefore, to see the significance of all this. There are many in the church today who would have us believe that so long as a man says, 'I am a Christian, I believe in Christ,' all is well and you do not ask him any questions at all. That is not the position of the apostle Paul. He says, in effect, 'It is not a matter of indifference as to whether Christ really did rise in the body on the morning of the third day or not. To me,' he says, 'it is not a matter of indifference as to whether Christ merely goes on living in a spiritual sense and never really came out of the grave and appeared and showed himself to his disciples and to certain chosen witnesses, and then ascended in their presence. To me it is absolutely vital, and there must be no uncertainty about this at all.'

So it is not a matter of indifference; it is not enough just to say that though Christ was crucified on the cross, he still goes on living and can still influence us in this world in a spiritual sense. The gospel of the New Testament, the message of the Christian church from the beginning, is one which is based on the literal physical resurrection of the Son of God from the grave. It is based on the empty tomb, on the literal historical fact of Christ risen in the body from the dead.

And this is vital, as the apostle here emphasises, from the practical standpoint. Its importance emerges as we see the effect of wrong doctrine upon our daily life and living. Do you notice his argument? He says, Why baptise for the dead, '... if the dead rise not at all? ... And why stand we in jeopardy ever hour?' (vv. 29–30). If I am risking my life and my reputation on this matter, as I am, says Paul, I am a fool if this fact of the resurrection is not a fact. 'I protest by your rejoicing which I have in Christ Jesus our Lord, I die daily' (v. 31). He was dying daily for the gospel, but he says, this is all wrong if that other doctrine is right. 'If after the manner of men I have fought with beasts at Ephesus, what advantageth it me, if the dead rise not? let us eat and drink; for tomorrow we die' (v.32). So let there be no mistake about all this, says the apostle. What a man believes does matter; what a man believes in detail does count.

And it is as true in the church today as it was when Paul penned those words. What a man believes is ultimately going to determine his life. A man who is loose in doctrine eventually becomes loose also in his life and in his behaviour. And I do not hesitate to say that the church of God on earth is as she is today primarily because of the looseness of belief in doctrine which entered in the last century, and has continued to the present time. You cannot separate these things; doctrine and conduct are indissolubly linked. That is why the apostle writes the chapter and fights as he does for the truth of this particular doctrine.

Let us, therefore, see why all this is true and how it works out. Why must we believe in the New Testament doctrine of the literal physical Resurrection? I will give you a number of answers to that question. The first is that it is the one thing, above everything else, which really proves that Jesus of Nazareth is the eternal Son of God. I do not want to concentrate on this now, as we are more concerned with the practical aspects of the letter. But let us be clear about this. He was 'declared to be the Son of God with power, according to the spirit of holiness, by the resurrection from the dead' (Rom 1:4). It was the Resurrection that finally convinced the disciples, who hitherto had been uncertain and doubtful and sceptical. They were crestfallen and dejected because of the death on the cross. It was when they knew that he had risen, that they knew he was the Son of God. The Resurrection is the final ultimate truth of the unique deity of the Lord Jesus Christ. It is the ultimate certainty of the fact that he is indeed the only begotten Son of God.

And that, of course, leads to this: it substantiates his claim that he had been sent into the world by the Father to do a particular work. He kept on saying that; it is the great theme of John 17. He had been sent into the world by the Father to do a given work, and here, by the Resurrection, he proves that he has done the work, and completed it. Paul says in Romans: 'Who was delivered for our offences, and was raised again for our justification' (Rom 4:25). If the Lord Jesus Christ had not literally risen physically from the grave, we could never be certain that he had ever really finished the work. And what was the work? It was to satisfy the demands of the law. The law of God demands that the punishment for sin shall be death, and if he has died for our sins, we must not only be certain that he has died, but that he has finished dying, and that there is no longer death. He has answered the ultimate demands of the law, and in the same way he has answered all the ultimate demands of God. The argument of the New Testament is that when God raised his Son from the dead, he was proclaiming to the whole world, I am satisfied in him: I am satisfied in the work he has done. He has done everything. He has fulfilled every demand. Here he is risen – therefore I am satisfied with him.

Not only that. The Resurrection proved that he has conquered every enemy that was opposed to him, to God, and to us. He has not only satisfied the law and conquered death and the grave, he has vanquished the devil and all his forces, and hell and all the principalities and powers of evil. He has triumphed over them all, and he proves it in the Resurrection. The devil cannot hold him; death and hell cannot hold him. He has mastered them all; he has emerged on the other side. He is the Son of God, and he has completed the work which the Father had sent him to do.

And all this, of course, is of vital importance to us. It is only in the light of the Resurrection that I finally have an assurance of my sins forgiven. It is only in the light of the Resurrection that I ultimately know that I stand in the presence of God absolved from guilt and shame and every condemnation. I can now say with Paul, 'There is therefore now no condemnation to them which are in Christ Jesus' (Rom 8:1) because I look at the fact of the Resurrection. It is there that I know it.

You notice how Paul argues in 1 Corinthians 15:17 when he says, 'If Christ be not raised, your faith is vain; ye are yet in your sins.' If it is not a fact that Christ literally rose from the grave, then you are still guilty before God. Your punishment has not been borne, your sins have not been dealt with, you are yet in your sins. It matters that much: without the Resurrection you have no standing at all. You are still uncertain as to whether you are forgiven and whether you are a child of God. And when one day you come to your death-bed you will not know, you will be uncertain as to where you are going and what is going to happen to you. 'Who was delivered for our offences, and was raised again for our justification' (Rom 4:25). It is there in the Resurrection that I stand before God free and absolved and without a fear and know that I am indeed a child of God. So you see the importance of holding on to this doctrine and why we must insist upon the details of doctrine, and not be content with some vague general belief in the Lord Jesus Christ?

'But wait a minute,' I can imagine someone saying. 'Yes I believe all that, but my problem is, how am I to live in this world? You announce that great doctrine to me, but I am still confronted by the world, the flesh and the devil, and how am I going to meet that? My problem is, how to be sanctified, how to become holy; how to advance in grace and in the knowledge of God, and to follow Christ as I want to do?' Well, the answer to it all is given here in 1 Corinthians 15:19 – 'If in this life only we have hope in Christ, we are of all men most miserable', together with the other verses I have already quoted to you – verses 13, 32, 33. All these have a very practical effect upon our lives in this world.

Let me summarise all this. If we are concerned about our life in this world, and the fight against the world, the flesh and the devil, the first thing we must do, says the apostle, is to take an overall look at this great doctrine of the Resurrection of our Lord. The important thing always is not to be content only with considering your own particular sins. We have been emphasising that a good deal in considering this matter of sanctification, and we have seen that most people are defeated because they start with their own particular sin – the thing that gets them down. And, of course, they cannot get away from it: they are held captive by it. No, says Paul, the way to deal even with that particular problem is to turn your back upon it for the moment, and to look at the whole general situation and see yourself as a part of it, in this world.

The Lord Jesus Christ, according to this teaching, came into the world because of this problem of sin and evil: that is the whole meaning of the Incarnation. He came in order to fight the kingdom of darkness, the kingdom of sin, and of Satan. That was the whole purpose of his coming. Not only did he come to do that, he has succeeded in doing it. He was tempted of the devil, and he repulsed him every time: he mastered him. He defeated and conquered the devil and all his powers and all the forces of Hades. And he has finally done so in his death and in his glorious resurrection.

'Yes, that is all very well,' says our questioner, 'but after all, when I look around me I do not seem to see that. I see sin and temptation flagrant, rampant. I see men intent upon evil. I see wars and hear of rumours of wars. It is all very well for you to say that Christ has conquered all these powers, but I do not see that in this world. How is all you are saying really going to help me?'

The answer is here in verses 23-25. 'But every man in his own order: Christ the first fruits; afterward they that are Christ's at his coming. Then cometh the end, when he shall have delivered up the kingdom to God, even the Father; when he shall have put down all rule and all authority and power. For he must reign, till he hath put all enemies under his feet.'

Now this means that the Lord Jesus Christ is still continuing the fight. When he was on earth in his own person he defeated the enemy at every point, and he finally routed and defeated him on the cross and in the Resurrection. Yes, but now having ascended up into heaven, he has led captivity captive, and is seated on the right hand of God's throne and authority and power. And what is he doing there? Well, according to this teaching, he is reigning there. This world has not got out of hand. It is still God's world, and Christ is still ruling and reigning over it. All authority is in his hands. He has been able to open the Book of history and the Book of destiny. He alone was strong enough to break the seals and to open the Book. So what we are taught by the Resurrection is that Christ is still there bringing his own purpose to pass.

We do not understand it all; we do not understand why he did not immediately bring it all to an end, but he has chosen not to do so. He has chosen to save a certain number of people; the fullness of the Gentiles and the fullness of Israel have got to come in. But this is the thing that is certain: as certainly as Christ rose triumphant over the grave, he is reigning at this moment, and he will reign until the time comes for him to return. The Lord Jesus Christ is going to come back into this world, and finally take the devil and all his forces, and cast them into a lake burning with fire. Evil and sin and wrong, and everything that is opposed to God, are going to be destroyed completely, and Christ will hand back a perfect kingdom to his Father. It is absolutely certain: he must reign, he will reign, until all his enemies have been put beneath his feet.

Now we must start with that. Our tendency is to be frightened by the devil and by temptation and the power and the forces of evil. 'Ah,' we say, 'how can a man, a weak man, fight against all that?' I say, look away from yourself for a moment; look at what is coming. He is reigning; he rules, and he is finally going to rout his enemies, and end it all. That is the general picture.

But let me show you the argument in a slightly more personal manner. How do I apply all that to my own case? I do so in this way. In a spiritual sense I am already risen with Christ: we have seen that in our previous studies. I am in Christ and Christ is in me. I am to reckon myself to be dead indeed to sin, and alive unto God. I have died with Christ; I have been buried with him; and I have risen with him. As a new man, I am in Christ, and as a new man in Christ I have risen; I have finished with death. I have got to die physically, but I have finished with the condemnation of death, and the terror and the sting of death have been taken out, as far as I am concerned. I am risen with him already spiritually.

But here I want to emphasise this other aspect. I am already risen with him spiritually, but I am yet going to rise with him in a physical and in a literal sense. 'For as in Adam all die, even so in Christ shall all be made alive. But every man in his own order: Christ the firstfruits, afterward they that are Christ's at his coming ...' (vv. 22–23), and then all the others. The resurrection of Christ, and the fact of the resurrection of Christ, is a certain, absolute announcement and proclamation that you and I and all people likewise rise from the grave in the body. The apostle explains how it all happens in the later portion of this great chapter – read it for yourselves, it is all there. 'We shall all be changed' (v.51). It will not be flesh and blood. There will be a change in 'the twinkling of an eye'. But we are all going to rise as the Lord Jesus Christ rose from the grave on that third morning. There will be some people left on earth when the Lord comes and they will be changed; it comes to the same thing.

But what does all this mean? Let me tell you what the Scripture says, and you will see its significance in the matter of our sanctification, and in the matter of our daily living. What I do know is that we shall all appear before the Judgement Throne of Christ, and give an account of the deeds done in the body, whether good or bad. And let me remind you, Christian people, that that is true of you and of me. Every one of us who is a Christian will have to appear before that Throne and give an account. But you see now the significance of the doctrine of the Resurrection: 'Evil communications corrupt good manners.' A man who realises every day of his life that he has got to stand before Christ and give an account, is a man who is very soon going to pay attention to the way he is living.

We shall all appear before him, and not only that, we read in 1 John 3:2 that, 'We shall see him as he is.' What a tremendous thought that is! Here on earth we have spent our time reading about him, thinking and meditating concerning him, but then we shall see him as he is. 'Now we see through a glass darkly, but then face to face' (1 Cor 13:12). Do you realise that? It is the Resurrection which tells you that – his resurrection, your resurrection. Furthermore, the next phrase in 1 John 3:2 tells us that we shall be like him. Paul says here in 1 Corinthians 15:53 that we shall be incorruptible – 'This corruptible must put on incorruption' – and in Philippians 3:21 he tells us that the Lord will return and that he 'shall change our vile body [the body of our humiliation] that it may be fashioned like unto his glorious body, according to the working whereby he is able even to subdue all things unto himself.' My very body shall be changed; I shall be incorruptible; I shall be glorified; I shall be like him even in my body. What a staggering thought!

And then beyond all that, these Scriptures tell us that we shall spend our eternity in his glorious presence. We shall be with him, with God, with Christ, with the Holy Spirit, with the spirits of just men made perfect, with holy angels. Because we shall rise we shall go on and spend our eternity in that indescribable glory. That is what the Scripture tells us is the significance and the meaning of this doctrine of the Resurrection.

What, then, do I conclude from all this? What are the deductions that we must inevitably draw from all this if we really believe it? Well the first, surely, is that if that is true, then we must have nothing to do with this condemned world. If I really believe that this world is evil and that it belongs to Satan, I must believe the apostle when he says that Christ must reign until he has put all his enemies under his feet. 'Then cometh the end, when he shall have delivered up the kingdom to God, even the Father; when he shall have put down all rule and authority and power' (1 Cor 15:24). The New Testament message is that the

world is controlled by the devil and by hell. Worldliness is evil
– the lust of the flesh and the lust of the eye and the pride of life.
It is all evil; it is all under condemnation. It is going to be
destroyed, utterly and completely. If we believe all this, can we
still desire that? Do we still want it? Do we regard the gospel that
tells us to turn our backs upon it all as narrow? What interest can
we possibly have in it?

My dear friends, we are inconsistent, we are false, if we say
one thing and do the other. We are contradicting our own doctrine. If we really believe this message, how can we desire the
world, and how can we enjoy it? It is to be destroyed, and if we
belong to it we shall be destroyed with it. 'Evil communications
corrupt good manners.' Those who really believe this doctrine
that we have been looking at together will not want to compromise with that world which is under condemnation, and
with evil and sin. I do not understand it when I see people who
call themselves Christian attaching great significance to worldly
position and worldly pomp and power, to things that belong to
the realm of the condemned, to the realm of evil. There is nothing of that in the New Testament. We are all one before Christ,
every one of us. Whatever we may happen to be by birth or position, we are all sinners, we are all under judgement, we are all
condemned by the law. We have nothing to do with those
worldly things, and if we believe this doctrine we must turn our
backs upon them all, whatever may be the consequences. That
is the first inevitable deduction.

The next thing I deduce is that it is our business and our duty
always to keep our eyes on the ultimate. Half our troubles are
due to the fact that we fail to do so. We are always looking at this
sin of ours, this thing that gets us down today. But we must
look at the ultimate. We must keep our eyes on the eternal. 'For
our light affliction, which is but for a moment, worketh for us
a far more exceeding and eternal weight of glory; while' – and
only while – 'we look not at the things which are seen, but at the
things which are not seen …' (2 Cor 4:17–18). Does that sin get
you down? Have you been praying to be delivered from it and
yet are still committing it? Well, let me give you a piece of

advice. Stop praying about it; rather, remind yourself that you are going to die, and that after death you will rise from the dead, and that you will stand before the Judgement seat of Christ, that you are going to look into his face – into his eyes – and that you are going to 'see him as he is'. And then if you can still go on doing that particular thing, I do not understand it. That is how the New Testament tells you to face your particular sin: just put it into the light of this ultimate doctrine. Realise that you call yourself a Christian, and all that that means, and what it is going to mean. Put everything into the light of that.

My third deduction is that having looked thus at the ultimate, we must never be discouraged. Oh, I am going further still – we have no right to be discouraged. It is a sin to be discouraged. A discouraged Christian is a contradiction in terms; he is denying his Lord. We must not be discouraged, because we are not left to ourselves. He is there seated at God's right hand. He is reigning, and he has said, 'All power is given unto me in heaven and in earth' (Mt 28:18). Do you not know, says Paul, writing to the Ephesians, the power that works in you? It is 'his mighty power, which he wrought in Christ, when he raised him from the dead' (Eph 1:19–20). You have no right to be discouraged. He, unseen, is still with us, bringing his purposes to pass, forming his kingdom, gathering out his elect, working it all to that ultimate end. We are not left to ourselves.

Then there is this great word with which Paul ends 1 Corinthians 15 – 'Therefore my beloved, be ye stedfast, unmoveable, always abounding in the work of the Lord, forasmuch as ye know that your labour is not in vain in the Lord.' It cannot be, in the light of this ultimate fact. It does not matter very much what men may say of you; it is what the Lord thinks that matters. Men may laugh at you, they may deride you, they may dismiss you, they may forget all about you, and of course, if you are thinking in terms of time, that is very serious. If you are only thinking of this world, then the greater the praise you get from men the better for you. Our Lord said about people like that: 'Verily I say unto you, They have their reward' (Mt 6:2). It is the only reward they are going to get – the praise of men in this passing, temporary world. But if you know that you are a child of God and that you are going to stand before him and see him face to face, the only thing that is going to count with you is what he thinks, not what anybody else thinks. Do not be discouraged.

Then I draw this fourth deduction: that the world cannot separate me from him and from his love. 'For I am persuaded, that neither death, nor life, nor angels, nor principalities, nor powers, nor things present, nor things to come, nor height, nor depth, nor any other creature, shall be able to separate us from the love of God, which is in Christ Jesus our Lord' (Rom 8:39). I have despaired of myself a thousand times, and my only hope at such times is that though I cannot see anything in myself, he has loved me and has died for me, and will never let me go. I am certain of it.

But I also draw this deduction: if all this is true – and it is – then I have no time to lose or to spare. I shall see him as he is. I shall be like him. I shall stand before that Judgement Throne of his. Have I got time to waste in these days and in this world? The days and the weeks, the months and the years are slipping through my fingers. I will be dead before I know where I am. I have not a moment to waste. If I believe I am going there, it is about time that I began to prepare. If you knew you were going to have an audience at Buckingham Palace in a week, you would be getting ready, would you not? You would be preparing your clothing, and your appearance, and rightly so. If, therefore, you are going to face the King of kings and the Lord of lords and have an audience with him, have you a second to spare? 'Every man that hath this hope in him, purifieth himself, even as he is pure' (1 Jn 3:3). If you do not want to feel ashamed of yourself, and feel that you are a cad when you stand and look into his blessed holy face, and see the marks of the nails, and the wound in his side, which he suffered for you, then prepare for the sight of him, prepare yourself to meet him.

Then, above and beyond everything else, let us dwell upon the glory of it all. Here we are still in this sinful world, and there are so many discouragements, and people may misunderstand us, and things seem to go against us. My friends, do not look at them. 'While we look not at the things which are seen, but at the things which are not seen: for the things which are seen are temporal; but the things which are not seen are eternal' (2 Cor 4:18). Oh, that the Holy Spirit might open our eyes! If we could but see something of them: 'The things which God hath prepared for them that love him' (1 Cor 2:9). The vision of God! To be with Christ! The ineffable purity and holiness of it all: the joy and the singing and the glory! No sighing, no sorrow, no tears, all that left behind: perfect, unmixed, unalloyed glory and happiness and joy and peace. The Resurrection tells us that if we belong to Christ we are going on to that.

So, then, this is the last conclusion, 'Awake to righteousness, and sin not' (1 Cor 15:34). The trouble, says Paul, is that 'some have not the knowledge of God: I speak this to your shame.' The real trouble with a man who is living a life of sin, and who is not sanctified, is that he lacks the knowledge of doctrine. That is his trouble: he does not know these things. And if you and I are not more determined than ever to 'awake to righteousness' and to forsake sin, then the only explanation is that we do not believe the doctrine of the Resurrection. And if we do not, we are yet in our sins and are destined for hell, and may God have mercy on us.

But then to crown it all, in the last verse of this chapter 15 Paul uses the word 'Therefore'. That is the argument, you see the logic – you cannot get away from it. It is not just beautiful language. You have heard people revelling in a beautiful service, and saying, 'How marvellous, how beautiful, how perfect – the balance and the cadence and the lilt of the words!' But that is not what the apostle wants you to feel. He wants you to say this, 'Therefore' – 'Therefore, my beloved brethren, be ye stedfast, unmoveable.' Let them say what they like about you: stand on your doctrine like a man, unmoveable. It is the doctrine of God; it is eternal. Stand steadfast, unmoveable, 'always abounding in the work of the Lord'. In your personal life and living, in your life in the church and for him, in your personal witness and testimony, in the whole of your life – 'abounding!' 'Forasmuch as

ye know that your labour is not in vain in the Lord.' The doctrine of the Resurrection. What a stimulus to our sanctification!
Let nothing come between us and all this mighty truth that
we have been considering together. This is vital. This is life.
This is everything.

Love so amazing, so divine
Demands my soul, my life, my all.

*Isaac Watts*